✠

The Man of Sorrows

✠

The Man of Sorrows

A Book of Lenten Devotions on the Passion of Our Lord

By

Albert T. W. Steinhaeuser

Minneapolis
Augsburg Publishing House

Publishers' Note

Few fields of Christian literature and art are so rich
as that of the Passion of our blessed Lord—His sufferings, crucifixion, death, and burial. This may in part
be accounted for by the fact that the sheer drama of
the events has provided great writers and artists with
unlimited material. But the deep reason is that the Passion of Jesus Christ deals with the fundamental relation of a just and merciful God to the sinful children
of His creation. To it the best artists and greatest writers of the Christian age have devoted their highest
talents.

Through the meditations and prayers in *The Man
of Sorrows,* A. T. W. Steinhaeuser tells the simple story
of the Passion which inspires to adoration, thanksgiving, and supplication. The added prayers and litanies
are culled from the Christian devotional literature of
all time.

This completely new edition of *The Man of Sorrows*
is presented with the prayer that this Lenten classic
will continue to bring the ageless message of the Crucified One to the hearts of its readers.

𝕿𝖍𝖊 𝕸𝖊𝖉𝖎𝖙𝖆𝖙𝖎𝖔𝖓𝖘 𝖆𝖓𝖉 𝕻𝖗𝖆𝖞𝖊𝖗𝖘 which here follow, since they are published in order to arouse the reader thereof to the love or fear of God or to self-examination, are not to be read in the midst of turmoil, but in stillness, not quickly but slowly, with close and serious consideration. Nor ought the reader to be careful to read through the whole of any one among them, but so much as he perceives may by God's help do him good in kindling within him the desire of prayer, or so much as may give him pleasure. Nor need he begin any one of them always at the beginning but wherever shall best please him. For to this end are they divided into paragraphs, that anyone may begin or leave off where he chooses; so that the length of a prayer or the frequent repetition of one thing may not become wearisome, but that the reader may gather thence some taste of devotion, for to that end were they composed.

(St. Anselm's Preface to his Meditations and Prayers)

From pain to pain, from woe to woe,
With loving hearts and footsteps slow,
To Calvary with Christ we go.
See His Precious Blood
At every Station pours!
Was ever grief like His?
Was ever sin like ours?

Contents

✠

The Man of Sorrows

✠

Prayer for a Good Lent

Father, the hour is come; glorify Thy Son:
That Thy Son may also glorify Thee.

Behold, now is the accepted time:
Behold, now is the day of salvation.

LORD JESUS CHRIST, Son of the living God, Who
for our redemption willedst to be rejected by the
Jews, betrayed with a kiss by Judas, seized, bound,
and led in bonds to Annas, Caiaphas, Herod, and
Pilate, and before them to be mocked, smitten
with palm and fist, with the scourge and the
reed; to have Thy face covered and defiled with
spitting, to be crowned with thorns, accused by
false witnesses, condemned, and led as an innocent Lamb to the slaughter, bearing Thine own
Cross; to be pierced through with nails, to have
vinegar and gall given Thee to drink, on the
Cross to die the most shameful of deaths, and to
be wounded with a spear: Do Thou by these Thy
most sacred pains deliver us from all sins and
penalties, and by Thy holy Cross bring us, miserable sinners, to that place whither Thou didst
bring with Thee the penitent robber on his late
repentance; Who livest and reignest with the Father and the Holy Ghost, One God, world without end. *Amen.*

God the Father bless me; God the Son defend
me; God the Holy Ghost preserve me, now and
for ever. *Amen.*

Ash Wednesday

The kings of the earth set themselves, and the rulers take counsel together: against the Lord, and against His Anointed.

Yet have I set my King: upon my holy hill of Zion.

Matthew 26:1-5

(Mark 14:1-2; Luke 22:1-2).

And it came to pass, when Jesus had finished all these words, He said unto His disciples, Ye know that after two days the passover cometh, and the Son of man is delivered up to be crucified. Then were gathered together the chief priests, and the elders of the people, unto the court of the high priest, who was called Caiaphas; and they took counsel together that they might take Jesus by subtlety, and kill Him. But they said, Not during the feast, lest a tumult arise among the people.

I

Our Lord's active ministry was ended, His ministry of suffering was about to begin. Since the day at Cæsarea Philippi He had predicted, in ever clearer terms, His Passion and death. The last prediction differed from those preceding in that it contained a definite date and was cast in the present tense. The Passion, He told His disciples, was to take place during

3

the week of the passover, which was but two days off. It was fitting that Christ, our Passover, should be sacrificed at this season, and equally fitting that Israel should crown its sin and complete its rejection of the Messiah upon its highest festival. The event was so near and so certain that He regarded it as already taking place—"the Son of man is delivered up to be crucified." Through the present tense, as through a window, shines the peace of God that filled His soul. He was aware of the plotting of His foes and the weakness of His followers, but behind and above bitter enemies and false friends He beheld the Father's will, which He was ready, now as always, to follow whithersoever it led. He could scarcely wait until He could say, "Father, the hour is come."

On the same day, but in striking contrast with Jesus and His quiet dependence upon God's will, the members of the Sanhedrin met in the house of Caiaphas to discuss how they might accomplish their own wicked will. They resolved, first, to seize and dispose of Jesus "by subtlety," and second, to take no action during the passover week. No time was wasted in debating whether or not Jesus was to be put to death—that had been decided upon long ago and was now taken up only as a piece of old, unfinished business. Since every open attempt to take Him had failed, they resorted to a policy of craft and intrigue. Their avoidance of the passover was not prompted by fear of desecrating so holy a season; what they were afraid of was a popular uprising. They would have liked best of all to carry out their purpose before the feast; but if the intervening interval should prove too short, they would resign themselves to wait as patiently as possible till the festival crowds had dispersed. Meanwhile they would keep eyes and ears open—who knew but there might come an inspiration from that master of subtlety, the murderer from the beginning! They did not have long to wait.

II

Thus, good Jesus, does Thy Passion begin. But has it not, in truth, begun long ago? The whole of Thy public ministry, what was it but a continuous Passion, from the Temptation in the wilderness onward? The devil departed from Thee "for a season," only to return again and again—in the fickleness of the multitude, in the hostility of the rulers, in the frailty of Thy followers. Thou didst marvel at the unbelief of Nazareth. Thou didst chide the blindness of Capernaum, Thou didst weep over Jerusalem's hardened heart. For days and weeks Thou wast in hiding from Thy foes, a fugitive and a vagabond in the earth. Didst not Thou choose the Twelve, and one of them was a devil? Even Peter the Rock became to Thee a stone of stumbling and sought to draw Thee from the way of the cross. So long time wast Thou with them, and yet they did not know Thee.

But still farther back, O my Lord, can I trace Thy Passion, even to the days of Thy holy childhood. A babe in Mary's arms, Thou wast carried by night to Egypt, out of reach of Herod's sword. In the temple, Thy parents understood not Thy saying, yet Thou wentest down with them to Nazareth and wast subject unto them. The shadow of the cross was upon all those hidden years. I see Thee as a child, running with arms outspread to Thy mother, and Thy shadow falls upon the ground, in form a cross. I behold Thee as man, standing in the doorway of the carpenter-shop, at close of a busy day, and wearily stretching out Thy arms; the sun casts Thy shadow on the floor, and I discern the outline of a crucified man. Yet, O Ancient of Days, to a far more distant past does Thy Passion extend. Art not Thou the Lamb slain from the foundation of the world? Thou art the same yesterday, and to-day, and forever. Thou wast in the beginning with God, and all things were made by Thee and for Thee. Even from everlasting, O Only-begotten Son, Thou wast in the bosom of the Father, planning in love Thy incarnation and atoning death, before ever these plotting priests and elders were known.

That was the prologue in heaven to the Passion, the accomplishment in time and space of opening verses, is the prologue on earth to the Passion which closed and crowned that life. Now begins the *Passio Magna,* the Great Passion which was Thy life. Here, in Matthew's gospel is found an account of the divine counsel of eternity. Open mine eyes, Lord Jesus, that I may behold wondrous things out of Thy suffering and death.

III

A LITANY OF REPENTANCE

O Lord, Who didst come to call sinners to repentance,
  Call them still and make them answer Thy call,

Be merciful to those who have no cloke for their sin,
But have seen and hated both Thee and Thy Father.

Thou Who didst melt the hardness of the thief,
Soften the hearts of all who are impenitent.

Thou Who didst recover the woman that was a sinner,
Recover all those who have fallen away from Thee.

Thou Who didst call Zacchaeus from the sycamore tree,
Arouse the careless and arrest the curious.

Thou Who didst speak the words of spirit and of life,
Enlighten the ignorant and teach the unlearned;
Dispel all prejudices, correct all errors;
Establish Thy people in the truth of the Gospel.

Thou Who didst call St. Matthew from the receipt of custom,
Deliver many souls from the slavery of the world.

Thou Who didst pray for Thy murderers,
Pity those who oppose Thy rule and persecute Thy servants.

Thou Who didst cast out many devils,
Set free many by the power of Thy grace, who are possessed
    by the devils of drink and lust.

Thou Who didst satisfy the doubts of St. Thomas,
Deal gently with those who can scarcely believe.

Thou Who didst uplift the sinking St. Peter,
Support all those who are weak and unstable.

Thou Who didst come to proclaim deliverance to captives,
Pity all prisoners and loose the chain of their sins.

Thou Who didst heal the impotent man,
Uphold those who are weakened by past sin.

7

Thou Who didst still the tempest on the lake,
  Rebuke the storms of passion and anger, and bid the waves
  be still.

Thou Who didst heal the withered hand,
  Recover for many the faculties which they have lost, of
  prayer and work, of self-control and self-sacrifice.

Thou Who didst make both the deaf to hear and the dumb
  to speak,
  Open deaf ears to Thy message;
  Loosen stammering tongues to speak words of penitence.

Thou Who didst put to shame the woman of Samaria,
  Reveal to many who are living in sin the shame of their life,
  and bring them to repentance.

Thou Who didst raise the dead to life,
  Quicken dead souls to the life of righteousness.

JESUS! JESUS! JESUS!

Who didst come to save Thy people from their sins,
  Save us, O Saviour!

HOSANNA!

For the Merits of Christ's Passion

O JESUS, my adorable Savior, behold me prostrate at Thy feet, imploring Thy mercy. Vouchsafe to apply to my soul the infinite merits of Thy Passion, on which I am now about to meditate. Grant that while I follow Thee along this Way of Sorrows, my heart may be so touched with true contrition, that I may be willing to accept cheerfully for Thy sake all the sufferings and humiliations of my pilgrimage on earth. *Amen.*

IV

"AH, TRAVELLER, WHY CHOOSE THIS WAY?"

"Ah, Traveller, why choose this way—
This rather than another?"
"This way man calls me, him I must obey,
For is he not my brother—
He only, and none other?"

"But, Traveller, why all this speed?
Such haste ends in undoing."
"If I should tarry now in his dire need,
Disgrace were mine and ruing—
And that were mine undoing."

"Then what is it Thou look'st to see
There at Thy journey's ending?"
"His feeble hands outstretched for help to me
Ere all is yet past mending,
And nothing left but ending."

"And what is it Thou think'st to hear—
Blessing or curses, crying?"
"If need be, both; it is not those I fear,
But that e'en now he's dying
With none to heed his crying."

"But to him is no smoother way
Than this Thy torn feet follow?"
"Others I've trod—in vain; by this I may
Be there to comrade him at end of day;
So, spite of hill and hollow,
This way I choose to follow."

✠

LORD, LET ME FEAR, LOVE AND TRUST IN THEE ALONE

The First Thursday

While the King sitteth at His table my spikenard sendeth forth the smell thereof.
For love is strong as death.

Matthew 26:6-13

(Mark 14:3-9; John 12:1-8).

Now when Jesus was in Bethany, in the house of Simon the leper, there came unto him a woman having an alabaster cruse of exceeding precious ointment, and she poured it upon His head, as He sat at meat. But when the disciples saw it, they had indignation, saying, To what purpose is this waste? For this ointment might have been sold for much, and given to the poor. But Jesus perceiving it said unto them, Why trouble ye the woman? For she hath wrought a good work upon me. For ye have the poor always with you; but me ye have not always. For in that she poured this ointment upon my body, she did it to prepare me for burial. Verily I say unto you, Wheresoever this gospel shall be preached in the whole world, that also which this woman hath done shall be spoken of for a memorial of her

I

While His foes were plotting His death, the friends of Jesus made Him a supper, and one of them, a woman, poured a box of precious ointment upon His head.

Her name is not given in Matthew nor in Mark, but from John we know that it was Mary, the sister of Martha, whose brother Lazarus Jesus had raised from the dead. The disciples found fault with her act, condemning it as wasteful folly. They estimated the value of the ointment if sold, and the good it might do if given to the poor. But Jesus said that no poor person need suffer because of Mary's deed. His followers could do good to the poor any day, but there was scant time left in which to do good to Him. Here again Mary chose "the good part," which should not be taken from her. As Jesus had been obliged, upon a former occasion, to defend her against her sister, who complained that she was not doing enough, He now defended her against His disciples, who blamed her for doing too much. While it was important to minister to Him, as Martha had done, it was more important to let Him minister, as Mary had done. So it was important now that the poor be not neglected, but it was infinitely more important that Jesus be not neglected. He therefore called Mary's act a good work, a beautiful deed, and interpreted it by reading into her gift all that it meant to Him. This is the only time He called anyone's work good, and it was the work not of busy Martha, but of Mary who sat at His feet and heard His word.

Mary may well have looked at Jesus in astonishment, for "the actions of holy persons often contain mysteries which they understand not themselves." Our Lord not only answers our prayers and gives us more than we asked or thought, He also accepts our gifts and finds

11

in them more than we gave or thought. As He is merciful to the sins of penitents, covering them and remembering them no more, so He is magnanimous toward the good works of believers, remembering and making much of them, and drawing out of their depths treasures they never dreamed were there.

What Mary's gift and work meant to Him, Jesus showed by taking it as the anointing of His body for burial, and by predicting in the some breath the triumphant march of His Gospel through the world. He considered Himself as good as dead and ready for the grave. But so long as devotion such as Mary's was found among men, His cause could not die. His death would give to the Gospel its saving content, and love like Mary's would keep it alive upon earth. Conversely, the Gospel would keep Mary's memory alive, and carry her example far and wide for the imitation of all.

II

Thou, O Jesus, art worthy to receive glory, and honor, and riches, and power. At the beginning of Thy life the wise men from the East spread before Thee their shining and fragrant gifts. At its close Mary of Bethany broke her alabaster box and poured her ointment over Thy head, so that the house was filled with the odor. I have nothing so rich and fine; yet if, like Mary, I bring my best, my gift will be as precious as hers. If I do what I can, Thou wilt do with it what Thou alone canst, Thou wilt ennoble and enrich it by Thy acceptance. Whatever it is in itself, as it passes from my hands to Thine it will turn to pure gold. Like

St. Andrew's little lad, I may see my five barley loaves
and few small fishes become a banquet for thousands.

I cannot bring my gifts to Thee directly. Thou hast
gone away, but Thy poor are with me always. In them
I can anoint Thy feet. Are not the poor Thy feet, good
Jesus, wherewith Thou comest to me and standest at
my door? Thou hast said that whatsoever we do unto
the least of Thy brethren, we do it unto Thee. O
blessed poor! for yours is the kingdom of heaven. O
blessed all ye merciful! for ye shall obtain mercy.

Let me not forget who it was that performed that
"good work," nor in what school the art of it was
learned. It was not Martha, who served, but Mary,
who sat at Thy feet. O my Lord, who camest not to
be ministered unto, but to minister! forbid that I
should be careful and troubled about many things, and
lose the one thing needful. Let me not listen to those
who would reproach me for giving myself continually
to prayer and to the Word, for spending much time
in the secret place behind the shut door, for lavish-
ing precious gifts upon my Lord. Let me fly from
such voices to Bethany, and give heed to Thy words
—"Mary hath chosen the good part: Mary hath
wrought the good work." Let me ever put the good
part first. First Thou must sow in my heart the living
seed of Thy Word; then only can there be fruit. First
there must be faith, the gift of God, that cometh by
hearing; then only can the good work follow. First
Thou must say to me, "This have I done for thee";
then only canst Thou ask, "What wilt thou do for me?"
First it must be, "He first loved us"; then, "we love."

13

III

For Faith That Worketh by Love

My jesus, Who for me didst give Thy self, Thy all, grant me to love above all else to sit at Thy pierced feet and hear Thy Word. I would hear as from Thine own lips the story of Thy Love. I would hide Thy Word in my heart. There let it burn and glow, and quicken in me a living faith. And let this faith, kindled at Thy love, be a faith that worketh by love, an active, eager, tireless thing, that asks not if good works should be done, but has done them long before the question can be asked, and is ever doing them gladly. Grant this for Thine own sake. *Amen.*

An Act of Love

O lord, thou art love, and because Thou art Love, and hast first loved me, I love Thee with all my heart. I love Thee for Thine own infinite perfections, and for all Thy love to me. I love Thee in Thy Word, and will gladly hear and learn it. I love Thee in Thy Blessed Sacrament, and will receive it in true faith. I love Thee in Thy Church, which is Thy Body, in which I will faithfully bear my part. I love Thee in my neighbor, and will help and comfort him in danger and want. I love Thee in Thy poor, whom I will give food and drink, and clothe and visit for Thy sake. O good Lord, make me day by day to love Thee more and more. *Amen.*

Against Harsh Judgment

LORD JESUS, everywhere and always inspire us to refuse the evil and to choose the good; and, we beseech Thee, give us grace never to judge our neighbor rashly, while one by one we ourselves endeavor to learn and perform Thy will; for Thine own Name's sake. *Amen.*

IV

"LO, CHRIST HATH GONE TO BETHANY"

Lo, Christ hath gone to Bethany,
    And Simon hath prepared the board;
Amid that blessed company
    There let us stand and see the Lord,

What doth the busy Martha seek?
    Is that the dead doth sit and eat?
But where is Mary—she so meek?
    She leaneth o'er her Saviour's feet.

Hanging her locks, in holy fear,
    She opes the odorous nard, 'tis she,
O'er His blest head, and far and near
    'Tis fragrant with her piety.

Oh, let not whispering envy blame,
    Nor avarice in wisdom's guise,
The anointing of the dying Lamb
    For His approaching obsequies.

Where o'er the earth, from clime to clime,
    The messenger of peace shall call,
So far shall bear recording time
    Meek Mary's blest memorial.

15

THE MAN OF SORROWS

Then may we bless Him without blame,
    The Father, Son, and Spirit's Name,
The Son who came meek Mary's Guest,
Who now in Him hath endless rest.

☩

GOOD JESUS MAKE ME WHOLLY THINE,

AND TEACH ME TO PLEASE THEE

The First Friday

---

*Mine enemies speak evil of me: When shall he die,
and his name perish?*

*Yea, mine own familiar friend, in whom I trusted,
who did eat of my bread: hath lifted up his heel
against me.*

Matthew 26:14-16

(Mark 14:10-11; Luke 22:3-6)

Then one of the twelve, who was called Judas Iscariot,
went unto the chief priests, and said, What are ye
willing to give me, and I will deliver Him unto
you? And they weighed unto him thirty pieces of
silver. And from that time he sought opportunity to
deliver Him unto them.

I

The offer of Judas to the chief priests follows closely,
in Matthew and Mark, upon the anointing at Bethany.
Now we know, even apart from John's statement,
who was the ringleader of the opposition to Mary's
deed. A light falls also upon the immediate occasion
of the betrayal. It was not so much the rebuke that
Jesus administered, as His quiet acceptance of the
anointing as His preparation for the grave. This, then,
was the meaning of His many predictions of the Passion! He was actually reckoning with their literal ful-

17

fillment and looking forward to His imminent death and burial; there was to be no resistance, no evasion of the crisis! Here was the end of Judas's hopes. Instantly his greed leaped to its feet, and he resolved to turn the inevitable to his own advantage. His disappointment and his love of money joined hands and made of the disciple a traitor.

Thus he burst in upon the perplexed councilors with his thrice welcome offer. Matthew records his words in their most sordid and mercenary form—"How much will you give me if I betray Him to you?" In order to bring out more vividly the greed of Judas and the eagerness of the priests, he portrays the latter as not merely promising the money, but actually weighing it out then and there—so anxious were they to seal the bargain. The transaction is reported in the same words in which an old prophet described the dismissal of the shepherd of Jehovah with the paltry wage of thirty pieces of silver. This was the prescribed price of a slave and expressed the contempt in which the leaders of the flock, then and now, held their God and those whom He had sent. It was, as the Lord told His prophet with bitter irony the "goodly price" at which His people valued Him.

How glad the priests were at this turn of events! We can see them smiling and rubbing their hands. Their plan to take Jesus "by subtlety" was about to be realized, and their reluctant decision "not during the feast" could at once be amended to read "at the first favorable opportunity." They laughed at their former fears; Jesus was not so dangerous a person as they had thought. If His own disciple turned against Him, there need be little fear of trouble from the populace. That night, for the first time in many weeks, those priests and elders slept in peace. But for Judas there was no sleep now, no rest. Henceforth his life held but one purpose—to earn the traitor's wage.

II

Who can unravel the tangled skein of motives in this man's breast? One, however, stands out plainly enough —the love of money. John calls Judas a thief, and declares that he pilfered from the common fund. This seems indeed to have been his besetting sin. Truly, money is the mammon of unrighteousness, and the love of it a root of all evil. This sin also Thou tookest upon Thee, Thou spotless Lamb. How it must have grieved Thee to see Thy familiar friend and disciple fall into this temptation and snare! On him Thy precept and example were thrown away. Thy parables of the Unjust Steward, of Dives and Lazarus, and of the Rich Fool left him unmoved. He beheld the young ruler go away grieved, because he had great possessions; he heard Thee say that they who have riches shall hardly, with much difficulty and only by a divine miracle, enter into the kingdom; he smiled at Thy graphic figure of a clumsy camel attempting to slip through an opening narrow enough for comparison with a needle's eye. And he sold his Lord for paltry money! O my Lord, let me never forget the shameful part played in Thy Passion by the love of money. Let me find the right relation to my worldly possessions, be they many or few. Am I their master or their slave? Do I make friends by means of them, or do they make me false to my friends and a traitor to the best Friend of all? Are they to me a means of doing good, or do they draw me away to selfishness and pride, to avarice and treachery? O Jesus, betrayed for filthy lucre! remove out of my heart every mercenary thought, every covetous desire, every wish to withhold more than is meet. Let me not forget to do good and to communicate. Set me as Thy steward over all my goods.

Judas sought a favorable opportunity to deliver his Lord. He lay awake at night pondering this thought, it was uppermost in his mind all day long. How hard men toil at their own undoing! What thought and ingenuity, what time and talents they spend upon evil! If they would turn the same energy into channels of usefulness, how much good they might do to others, and how much happier their own lives would be! Truly, the way of the transgressor is hard. Let me choose rather the narrow way; with all its hardships it is the way of peace and leads to endless joy. O good Jesus, there was more joy in Thy breaking heart on Calvary than in the heart of Judas with the thirty pieces jingling in his bag. Teach me to seek first God's kingdom and righteousness, then will all else be added unto me. Let me lay up for myself treasures in heaven; and where my treasure is, there will my heart be also.

III

Against Worldiness and Avarice

ALL HAIL, SWEET JESUS! Praise, honor, and glory be to Thee, O Christ, Who wast sold for paltry money by Thy faithless disciple, when the Jews were persecuting Thee and conspiring against Thy life. Root out, I pray Thee, from my heart every wrong desire for created things. Pardon me, O Holy Redeemer, for having so often preferred vain and perishing things to Thee, and turned myself away from Thee for worthless pleasures. O good Jesus, gracious Jesus! O my Hope, my Refuge, and my Salvation! Give me true humility, patience, charity, the government of my tongue, and control over my senses. Have mercy upon us all, and grant that we may neither rejoice in riches if we have them, nor repine after them if we have them not; but may trust only in the riches of that salvation which Thou hast obtained for all those who are willing to share Thy poverty. Father, Son, and Holy Ghost: glory be to Thee in all Thy people for ever. *Amen.*

Against Covetousness and Hypocrisy

O GOD, HEAVENLY FATHER, Who to redeem us didst deliver up Thine only Son to be betrayed by one of His disciples and sold to His enemies: Take from us, we beseech Thee, all covetousness and hypocrisy, and so help us that, loving Thee and Thy Truth above all else, we may remain steadfast in our faith even unto the end, and cleaving to Thee with all our heart, may at last attain to the inheritance of the saints in light; through Him Who ever liveth to make intercession for us, Jesus Christ our Lord. *Amen.*

For Power to Conquer a Besetting Sin

O MOST MERCIFUL GOD, who knowest my sinfulness and my weakness, the temptations which have most power over me, and the sin which doth most easily beset me: Have mercy upon me, and help me. Forgive me my many and great falls, and give me Thy grace to serve Thee more faithfully for the time to come; for the merits and through the mediation of my only Lord and Saviour Jesus Christ. *Amen.*

IV

"FOR WHAT WILT THOU SELL THY LORD?"

For what wilt thou sell thy Lord?
"For certain pieces of silver, since wealth buys the world's good word."
But the world's word, how canst thou hear it, while thy brothers cry scorn on thy name?
And how shall thy bargain content thee, when thy brothers shall clothe thee with shame?

For what shall thy brother be sold?
"For the rosy garland of pleasure, and the coveted crown of gold."
But thy soul will turn them to thorns, and to heaviness binding thy head,
While women are dying of shame, and children are crying for bread.

THIRTY PIECES OF SILVER

For what wilt thou sell thy soul?

"For the world." And what shall it profit, when thou shalt
have gained the whole?

What profit the things thou hast, if the thing thou art be so
mean?

Wilt thou fill with the husks of having the void of the might-
have-been?

✠

LORD OF MERCY, DEFEND US
FROM ALL WICKEDNESS

The First Saturday

Thou preparest a table before me in the presence of mine enemies: Thou anointest my head with oil; my cup runneth over.

Surely goodness and mercy shall follow me all the days of my life: and I will dwell in the house of the Lord for ever.

Mark 14:12-17

(Matt. 26:17-20; Luke 12:7-14)

And on the first day of unleavened bread, when they sacrificed the passover, His disciples say unto Him, Where wilt Thou that we go and make ready that Thou mayest eat the passover? And He sendeth two of His disciples, and saith unto them, Go into the city, and there shall meet you a man bearing a pitcher of water: follow him; and wheresoever he shall enter in, say to the master of the house, The Teacher saith, Where is my guest-chamber, where I shall eat the passover with my disciples? And he will himself show you a large upper room furnished and ready: and there make ready for us. And the disciples went forth, and came into the city, and found as He had said unto them: and they made ready the passover. And when it was evening He cometh with the twelve.

I

From Luke we learn that it was Peter and John whom Jesus sent to prepare the last passover. The narrative as given by Mark has about it a directness and realism that we owe doubtless to Peter, whose memoirs of Jesus form the basis of our second gospel. By turning it into the first person we have the tale as it came originally from Peter's lips. "He despatched two of us"— so he will have told the tale—"saying to us, 'Go into the city, and you will meet a man carrying a water-jar; follow him, and whatever house he goes into, tell the owner that the Teacher says, "Where is my room, that I may eat the passover with my disciples?" He will himself show you a large room upstairs, with couches spread, all in readiness. Prepare the passover for us there.' We went and found everything just as He had told us. So we prepared the passover, and when evening came He arrived with the Twelve." All is told from the viewpoint of Peter and his companion, including the final "He arrived," that is to say, "We had everything ready by evening, and while we waited, we saw Him coming along with the rest of the Twelve." Here is one of the many human elements in the Gospel through which the divine comes home to our business and bosoms.

But our evangelist, too, has a personal interest in the narrative. Mark appears to be moving upon familiar ground. There are good reasons for believing that it was in the house of his parents in Jerusalem that the last Supper was held. He was thus permitted to sketch into the Passion History the picture of his own home, just as he sketched, afterwards, his own portrait. If this supposition is correct, we can understand his lingering in loving detail over this incident in his gospel. What memories it must have evoked in his mind!

More significant, however, is the air of mystery that surrounds the whole proceeding. The secret instructions, the silent following of the water-carrier, the enquiry for the master of the house, the password "The Teacher," the request to see "my guest-chamber," the showing by the master personally of the upper room in complete readiness—all this has about it a touch of strangeness, almost of romance, that adds a vivid note of human interest to this sombre passover eve. The secrecy was made necessary by the watchful eye of Judas seeking an opportunity to betray his Lord. His task was not to be made too easy for him. The place of the passover was not to be revealed beforehand, lest he should come with the soldiers before Jesus' hour had struck. What pains our Lord was at, to obtain this last undisturbed evening with His loved ones, this little quiet nook in time and space! We can well understand the relief with which He said, as He took His place at the table, "With desire have I desired to eat this passover with you and before I suffer."

II

When one disciple falls another is raised up in his place. It is always so. When Simon Peter denies his Lord, another Simon is found to take up the cross. Now that Judas fails Him, this unknown disciple is ready with his upper room. He was doubtless well known among the early followers of Jesus, but to us he is less than a name. "Mr. So-and-So" Matthew calls him. But though his name is not known upon earth, it cannot be unknown in heaven. The beloved Teacher will not have forgotten to keep an upper chamber for him in His Father's house. Indeed, it is very probable that the good man's offer of his guest-room suggested to Jesus the beautiful figure of the house with the many mansions, in which He promised to prepare a place for His own. Thus He repaid His unknown friend for the use of his room.

"Where is my guest-chamber?" Have not I some quiet place for Thee, O heavenly Guest, where we may meet in intimate communion? A room where I may sit, like Mary, at Thy feet and hear Thy Word? A chamber, like Daniel's in old Babylon, with windows open toward Jerusalem? A little chamber on the walls, with table, stool, and candlestick, for my Prophet to bide? A closet into which I may go, and shut the door, and pray to my Father in secret? An upper room to which Thou mayest come with Thy "Peace be with thee," and show me Thy hands and Thy side, and send me forth, even as the Father sent Thee? A hushed retreat for meditation and prayer, where in the silence I hear Thy hand upon the latch and Thy voice calling, "Behold, I stand at the door, and knock; if any man hear my voice, and open the door, I will come in to him, and will sup with him, and he with me"; where comes Thy whisper, "Open to me; for my head is filled with dew, and my locks with the drops of the night"; where I fling wide the door and cry, "Come in, Thou Blessed of the Lord; wherefore standest

27

Thou without?" Truly, good Jesus, Thou hadst not
where to lay Thy head. Like a thief in the night, like
one on mischief bent, Thou stealest through dark
streets and city lanes—only Thy errand is one of love.
Thou must meet plot with counterplot in order to find
a secluded place and snatch an unmolested hour in
which to keep Thy last passover, to institute Thy Holy
Supper. How hard men made it for Thee to do them
good! But hatred and treachery cannot daunt Thy love,
many waters cannot drown it. Thou hast foreseen this
hour and hast prepared for it. Thou hast Thy secret
friends and unknown meeting-places, Thy private
offers of help and hidden rooms. How calm Thou art,
how sure of everything—as sorrowful, yet always rejoicing; as poor, yet making many rich; as having
nothing, and yet possessing all things. In danger and
distress, O my Saviour, let the same quietness and
confidence be my strength; may I find in trust in God
and love to men my peace and hidden joy.

III

Komm, Herr Jesu, Sei Unser Gast

O WISE LOVE and loving Wisdom, Jesus the Divine Word, Who wast in the beginning with God,
and wast made flesh, and didst dwell among men;
Who didst endure the plotting of Thy foes, the treachery of Thine Apostle, the frailty of all Thy followers;
and Who, as Thou wast born in a stable, didst keep
Thy last passover in a friendly guest-room, and didst
lie at last in a stranger's grave: I adore Thee for Thy

homeless, wandering days, and I beseech Thee that Thou, Who now sittest at the right hand of God, wilt not disdain to come under my roof, unworthy though I am, even into my heart, where Thou wilt dwell by faith. Grant me, through Thy Holy Spirit, to make all things ready by true repentance and a lively faith, and do Thou bring with Thee, when Thou comest, all Thy precious merit and make it mine, O my King and my God. *Amen.*

For a Family

ALMIGHTY and Everlasting God, be Thou present to our duties, and grant the protection of Thy presence to all that dwell in this house; that Thou mayest be known to be the Defender of Thy family, and the Inhabitant of this dwelling; through Jesus Christ our Lord. *Amen.*

For the Homeless Poor

O LORD JESUS CHRIST, Who hadst not where to lay Thy head: Have mercy upon all those who are destitute of any earthly home. Thou hast borne their grief, pardon their sin. Give them the desire for industry and the opportunity of honest labor, that they may dwell peaceably upon the earth, until they come to those mansions which Thou hast provided in Thy Father's house for all who will return through Thee into the way of salvation; where, with the Father and the Holy Ghost, Thou livest and reignest, One God, world without end. *Amen.*

IV

LENTEN COMMUNION

Rest in a friend's house, Dear, I pray:
The way is long to Good Friday,
And very chill and gray the way.

No crocus with its shining cup,
Nor the gold daffodil is up,
Nothing is here save the snowdrop.

Sit down with me and taste good cheer:
Too soon, too soon, Thy Passion's here;
The wind is keen and the skies drear.

Lord, in the quiet, chill and sweet,
Let me pour water for Thy feet,
While the crowd goes by in the street.

Let us sit down and talk at ease
About Thy Father's business.
(What shouts were those borne on the breeze?)

So soon, so soon, the hour's flown!
The glory's dying: Thou art gone
Out on Thy lonely way, alone.

✠

LORD JESUS, COME TO ME,
THAT I MAY COME TO THEE

The First Monday

5. THE FOOT-WASHING

Have mercy upon me, O God, according to Thy loving kindness: according unto the multitude of Thy tender mercies blot out my transgressions.

Wash me thoroughly from mine iniquity: and cleanse me from my sin.

John 13:1-15

Now before the feast of the passover, Jesus knowing that His hour was come that He should depart out of this world unto the Father, having loved His own that were in the world, He loved them unto the end. And during supper, the devil having already put into the heart of Judas Iscariot, Simon's son, to betray Him, Jesus, knowing that the Father had given all things into His hands, and that He came forth from God, and goeth unto God, riseth from supper, and layeth aside His garments; and He took a towel and girded Himself. Then He poureth water into the basin, and began to wash the disciples' feet, and to wipe them with the towel wherewith He was girded. So He cometh to Simon Peter. He saith unto Him, Lord, dost Thou wash my feet? Jesus answered and said unto him, What I do thou knowest not now; but thou shalt understand hereafter. Peter saith unto Him, Thou shalt never wash my feet. Jesus answered him, If I wash thee not, thou hast no part with me. Simon Peter saith unto Him, Lord, not my feet only, but also my hands and my head. Jesus saith to him, He that is bathed needeth not save to wash his feet, but is clean every whit: and ye are clean, but not all. For He knew him that should betray Him; therefore

said He, Ye are not all clean. So when He had
washed their feet, and taken His garments, and sat
down again, He said unto them, Know ye what I
have done to you? Ye call me, Teacher, and, Lord:
and ye say well; for so I am. If I then, the Lord and
the Teacher, have washed your feet, ye also ought
to wash one another's feet. For I have given you an
example, that ye also should do as I have done to you.

I

By dint of long brooding on this incident John came
to see in it a dramatic parable of the Passion, setting
forth its humble spirit, its cleansing power, and its
salutary example. In this sense he presents it to his
readers, writing over it the title, "He loved His own
unto the uttermost."

In Jesus' kneeling before him with the basin and
the towel John beholds the Servant of Jehovah, who
came not to be ministered unto, but to minister, and
to give His life a ransom for many. Even so, being in
the form of God, He took upon Him the form of a
servant, and humbled Himself, becoming obedient
unto death, even the death of the cross. Peter could
not understand this, and thought it beneath his Master's dignity to perform this lowly service, when it was
in truth His highest glory, because it was the expression of His humble love.

As little could Peter comprehend the purpose and
the power of this love. He thought of bodily cleansing,
while Jesus' desire was to make His disciples "clean

every whit." Therefore He said to Peter, "If I wash thee not, thou hast no part with me." Afterwards Peter came to understand, as did John, that this was He that came by water and blood; not by water only, but by water and blood; and that the blood of Jesus Christ cleanseth us from all sin.

Least of all did Peter and the rest understand the example of Jesus' love. While the disciples were disputing which of them was the greatest, Jesus was in their midst as He that served. "I have given you an example"—thus He Himself summed up the meaning of the Footwashing—"that ye should do as I have done to you." What He had in mind was no mere outward repetition of an oriental custom, but the imitation of His humble, serving love. This is, as He said, His new—and only—commandment: "That ye love one another as I have loved you." It is a new commandment in that it sets up a new standard. The old commandment—"Thou shalt love thy neighbor as thyself"—put the standard of love within a man. In Jesus' commandment the standard is not within us, but without; it is in Jesus' love to the uttermost. We are to love one another as He loved us. This is Jesus' Golden Rule. Its observance is the certain mark of a true disciple.

II

Do I know, any better than Peter, what my Lord has done to me? On the lowest plane, am I as familiar as I should be with the historical events of the Passion? Do they stand out in my mind clearly and in

33

ordered sequence, from the Triumphant Entry on Palm Sunday to the Burial on Good Friday evening? Lord Jesus, let me use these Lenten days to read, mark, learn, and inwardly digest the story of Thy Love.

Mere intellectual knowledge, however, is not sufficient. The Holy Passion is more than a tale

> Of old, unhappy, far-off things
> And battles long ago.

It is history, but it is far more than history. It is the infinite and eternal love of God made real in time and space, and fastened by the cross of Jesus for ever to our earth. Do I know it in this sense? It is true, I cannot fathom the depth of His unsearchable riches. Yet it is possible to know the love of Christ, which passeth knowledge—to know it not with the groping intellect, but with the believing heart. Do I thus know my Saviour's love? At every station of the Cross do I hear the words, "For thee"? When I see Him washing His disciples' feet, instituting the Holy Supper, praying in the garden, betrayed and denied, mocked and scourged and crowned with thorns, crucified, dead and buried—can I say at every step of the Painful Way, "He loved me and gave Himself for me"? Good Jesus, grant me to know Thee as my Lord, who hath redeemed me, a lost and condemned creature, secured and delivered me from all sins, from death, and from the power of the devil.

But even that is not enough. I do not really know what He has done to me until I copy His example

and do to others as He has done to me. Sweetly sings
St. Bernard—

> The love of Jesus, what it is,
> None but His loved ones know

That is true, but it is not all the truth. He who is
only a loved one—even one of Jesus' loved ones—
knows but the half of love. Not until the loved one
has himself learned to love does he truly understand
what love means. When the love of Christ is shed
abroad in my heart, and becomes a living reality for
me, so that I experience something of the anguish
and the bliss of sacrifice for others, then only do I
know what He has done for me. I have come to the
highest knowledge attainable on earth. There remains
but the perfection of this knowledge in heaven. "Thou
shalt understand hereafter." Let me know Thee, Thou
Lover of souls; let me know Thee, and the power of
Thy resurrection, and the fellowship of Thy sufferings; let me know Thee now, and come hereafter to
the fulness of the knowledge of Thy Love.

III

"Wash Me, Saviour, or I Die"

Lord Jesus christ, Who in a wonderful parable
of Thy Passion didst wash Thy disciples' feet, wash
me, I pray Thee, that I may have part with Thee. O
Thou Who through the eternal Spirit didst offer Thyself without spot to God, grant that Thy Blood may
purge my conscience from dead works, to serve the
living God. Bless to me and mine the contemplation

of Thy Sufferings, that we may advance in knowledge
of Thy Love, and follow Thy mind in conduct worthy
of our calling. *Amen.*

A LITANY OF LOVE

O God the Father, Fountain of all being and of all love,
Who so lovedst the world as to give Thine Only-begotten
Well-beloved Son to die for us miserable sinners,

O God the Son, the Only-begotten Well-beloved Son, Who
for love of us, being God, becamest Man to save us, that
we might love Thee, being loved by Thee, everlastingly,

O God the Holy Ghost, Bond of the Love of the Father and
the Son, Who willest to shed abroad Thy Love into our
hearts,

Holy Trinity, One God Who art Love, have mercy upon
us, and fill us with Thy Love.

From the Enemy of our souls and of all love;

From all shadow of envy at the good of any;

From all painful thoughts that others may grudge me mine;

From dwelling on others' rudeness, or interpreting their words
amiss;

From an unquiet and discontented spirit;

From offence given or taken;

From gloominess and despondency;

From mistrust of Thee and of Thy mercies;

From fears and misgivings;

From any doubts of Thy boundless Love and tender Mercy
to me, Thy poor sinner;

Good Lord, deliver me, and fill me with the fulness of Thy
Love.

For the Love with which Thou hast ever loved me;

For the Love with which Thou didst create me to love me;

For Thy Mercy and Pity when I forgot Thee;

For recalling me to myself and to Thee;

For Thy forgiveness;

For all power of love, which by nature or by grace Thou
hast given me;

For all whom Thou ever gavest me to love me, or to be
loved by me;

For every motion of Thy grace whereby Thou didst call out
love in me;

For the benefits of Thy Love, with which, day by day, Thou
loadest me;

For every longing which Thou hast given me to love Thee
more;

For Thy readiness to hear whenever I call upon Thee;

For making me one with Thee, through Thine All-holy Body
and Blood;

   Give me, good Lord, love for love.

Charity, which suffereth long and is kind;

Charity, which envieth not;

Charity, which vaunteth not itself, and is not puffed up;

Charity, which doth not behave itself unseemly;

Charity, which seeketh not her own;

Charity, which is not easily provoked;

Charity, which thinketh no evil;

Charity, which rejoiceth not in iniquity, but rejoiceth in the
truth;

Charity, which beareth all things;

Charity, which believeth all things;

Charity, which hopeth all things;

Charity, which endureth all things;

Charity, which never faileth;

   Good Lord, increase, enlarge, perfect, fulfil in us to the end.

O God, Who hast prepared for them that love Thee such
good things as pass man's understanding: Pour into our
hearts such love toward Thee, that we loving Thee above all
things, and each other and all besides, in and for Thee,
may obtain Thy promises, which exceed all that we can
desire; through Jesus Christ our Lord. *Amen.*

IV

"I AM AMONG YOU AS HE THAT SERVETH"

O Blessed Jesus! when I see Thee bending,
  Girt as a servant, at Thy servants' feet,
Love, lowliness, and might, in zeal all blending,
  To wash their dust away, and make them meet
To share Thy feast, I know not to adore
Whether Thy humbleness or glory more.

Meek Jesus! to my soul Thy spirit lending,
  Teach me to live, like Thee, in lowly love;
With humblest service all Thy saints befriending,
  Until I serve before Thy throne above—
Yes! serving e'en my foes, for Thou didst seek
The feet of Judas in Thy service meek.

O blessed name of Servant; comprehending
  Man's highest honor in his humblest name;
For Thou, God's Christ, that office recommending,
  The throne of mighty power didst truly claim.
He who would rise like Thee, like Thee must owe
His glory only to his stooping low.

Daily my pilgrim feet, as homeward wending
  My weary way, are sadly stained with sin;
Daily do Thou, Thy precious grace expending,
  Wash me all clean without and clean within,
And make me fit to have a part with Thee
And Thine, at last, in Heaven's festivity.

✠

LORD, LET ME HAVE PART WITH THEE

The First Tuesday

6. THE TRAITOR UNMASKED

Search me, O God, and know my heart: try me and know my thoughts.
And see if there be any wicked way in me; and lead me in the way everlasting.

Matthew 26:20-25

(Mark 14:17-21; Luke 22:14, 21:23; John 13:21-30)

Now when even was come, He was sitting at meat with the twelve disciples; and as they were eating, He said, Verily I say unto you, that one of you shall betray me. And they were exceeding sorrowful, and began to say unto Him every one, Is it I, Lord? And He answered and said, He that dipped his hand with me in the dish, the same shall betray me. The Son of man goeth, even as it is written of Him: but woe unto that man through whom the Son of man is betrayed! Good were it for that man if he had not been born. And Judas, who betrayed Him, answered and said, Is it I, Rabbi? He saith unto him, Thou hast said.

I

Like a thunderclap from a clear sky came Jesus' announcement that one of the Twelve was going to betray Him. No wonder they were filled with dismay, and asked in their simple-hearted fashion, one by one,

39

"Lord, surely it is not I?" None of them would willingly commit this dreadful crime, yet they knew their frailty and proneness to evil. Only a few days before, their Master had found in Mary's heart impulses of devotion of which she scarcely dreamed. Now He was looking into their own hearts; did He see in them stirrings of evil of which they themselves were unaware?

Both Matthew and John introduce at this point incidents peculiar to their gospels. John, who leaned on Jesus' breast, records a private conversation with his Lord. "Lord," he whispered, "who is it?" and Jesus replied, "He it is to whom I shall give a sop when I have dipped it." Then John saw Him dip the sop and give it to Judas. Matthew also, who probably sat near Judas, observed something that escaped the rest. He alone heard the traitor's muttered question, "Surely it is not I, Rabbi?" and caught the full meaning of Jesus' reply, "Is it not?"

Besides being a piece of revolting hypocrisy, this question of the traitor sheds further light upon his motive. When he made his offer to the priests, disappointment and greed were uppermost in his mind. But underneath there may well have been a more subtle and deeply reasoned motive. A suggestion as to what this was appears in the close connection between his question and the words of Jesus that immediately preceded it. "It is true," said Jesus—as if replying to the unspoken argument of someone present—"it is true that my sufferings, including the betrayal, are foretold in Scripture; it is God's will and eternal plan. But that does not relieve the man who betrays me of personal responsibility. Let him not deceive himself. He can make no valid plea that he is a blind instrument in God's almighty hand. He is heaping up for himself such guilt and woe as will cause him to curse the day of his birth, and those who love him to regret that he ever saw the light."—"Surely you do not mean me, Teacher?" By this question the traitor betrayed himself. Jesus' constant emphasis upon the divine will behind His suffering—"all things written through the prophets shall be accomplished unto the Son of Man" —appears to have deeply impressed him. If these things must needs be, is it not well to have them soon over? If the dawn of His day of triumph is swiftly to follow the night of His crowning humiliation, why not hasten the hour of His vindication? Thus he stifled the voice of conscience and cloaked from his own sight the enormity of the crime which his own impatience to enter into his share of honor when Jesus should enter His Kingdom was driving him to commit. How well he succeeded is seen in the fact that even this final warning of Jesus fell on deaf ears.

II

O my good Lord, I would set before me the bitter sorrow with which Thou beheldest Thy chosen disciple turn traitor. At the time of his choosing there was in Judas that which made Thee covet him for Thine own—some gift of heart or mind that fitted him to be, no less than Peter and John and the others, one of Thy holy Apostles. Thy love dwelt on him no less richly than on them. But, alas ere long a change came over him, an evil spell seemed cast upon him, a coldness sprang up between disciple and Master. That day at Capernaum, when many of Thy followers went back and walked no more with Thee, Thou saidst to the Twelve, "Will you also go away?" Ah, if Judas had only gone away then; he would have escaped the greater condemnation. But he remained, and Thou saidst, "Have not I chosen you Twelve, and one of you is a devil?" What must it have cost Thee to watch this man drift day by day farther from Thee, to behold Satan crowding Thee slowly out of his heart! During that last week, to feel his furtive glance upon Thee, to see his hands clutching the price of blood, to know that of those the Father had given Thee this one Thou hadst lost, to taste at last his unclean kisses on Thy lips—was there bitterer drop than this in all Thy cup of woe?

How dark an abyss of evil is concealed in the human breast! "The heart is deceitful above all things, and desperately wicked: who can know it?" "Who can understand his errors? Cleanse Thou me from secret faults." I know not what hidden faults lie at the bottom of my heart, nor how soon they may rise to the surface. I know that I would not willingly grieve or offend my gracious Lord; yet I must confess, "The evil which I would not, that I do." Keep me, good Jesus, from pride and self-complacency, and from all judging of others. Even for Judas I would have pity rather than condemnation. Who am I to judge? Had I been twin to him in the mixture of my powers, and exposed to his temptations, who knows but I should have done the same as he? Nay, I know, and I confess, that I have many a time betrayed my Lord.

> O break, O break, hard heart of mine;
> Thy weak self-love and guilty pride
> His Pilate and His Judas were:
> Jesus, our Love, is crucified!

Let me watch always, and pray without ceasing. When I think I stand, let me take heed lest I fall. How many are called, how few chosen! He only that endureth unto the end shall be saved. He alone that is faithful unto death shall receive a crown of life. Be Thou to me Alpha and Omega, the beginning and the end, the first and the last. Give me, O Lord, the grace of perseverance. Grant me Thy mercy, that with my loins girded, and my light burning, I may await Thy coming, and be found worthy, through Thy grace, of the banquet of eternal life.

III

For Purity

O LORD, there is no hiding me from Thy presence, for if I should say, The darkness shall cover me, then shall my night be turned to day; for the darkness is no darkness with Thee, but the night is as clear as the day; the darkness and light to Thee are both alike. Therefore, O God, I present myself open before Thee;

O cleanse my soul, that I may rejoice to be seen of Thee in Christ Jesus. *Amen.*

Confession and Prayer for Pardon

O LORD JESUS CHRIST, Son of the living God, Who hast drained the cup of suffering for the salvation of all men, vouchsafe to grant me Thy help. Jesus most mild, I confess my own perverse iniquity. I was conceived and born in sin; Thou didst wash and sanctify me; and yet I have since defiled myself in deeper guilt. For my birth-sin was involuntary, my own defilements of my own free will. Behold, Lord, my wickednesses are gone over my head, and are like a sore burden, too heavy to be borne. And unless Thou, Whose property is ever to have mercy and to spare, wilt support me with the right hand of Thy majesty, I shall be swallowed up in the depths of misery. Hear me, O Lord my God, rescue my soul and save me for Thy mercies' sake. I beseech Thee, most loving Lord, record not against me my frowardness, and enter not into judgment with Thy servant, but according to the greatness of Thy mercy blot out mine offences. Stretch out Thine hand and save me from the hand of mine enemies. Sheltering under the shadow of Thy pity, I hasten to the throne of Thy glory, seeking pardon, crying and knocking until Thou have mercy upon me. Wherefore, O Jesus, arise, help me, and say to my soul, I am thy Salvation. Do Thou receive me, and draw me unto Thee, so that, being Thine by creation and redemption, I may abide in Thy likeness and in Thy love for ever. *Amen.*

For Self-Blame

Lord, ENLIGHTEN us to see the beam that is in our own eye, and blind us to the mote that is in our brother's. Let us feel our offences with our hands, make them great and bright before us like the sun, make us eat them and drink them for our diet. Blind us to the offences of our beloved, cleanse them from our memories, take them out of our mouths for ever. Let all here before Thee carry and measure with the false balances of love, and be in their own eyes and in all conjunctures the most guilty. Help us at the same time with the grace of courage, that we be none of us cast down when we sit lamenting amid the ruins of our happiness or our integrity: touch us with fire from the altar, that we may be up and doing to rebuild our city; in the name and by the method of Him in Whose words of prayer we now conclude.

OUR FATHER.

IV

BUT JUDAS WOULD NOT UNDERSTAND

When seated with Thy chosen band,
   Thou didst to Thy disciples say
   That one, O Christ, would Thee betray,
But Judas would not understand.

The sop revealed the traitor's hand,
   In answer to the question made;
   They saw by whom Thou wert betrayed,
But Judas would not understand.

The Jews, O Christ, Thy life demand,
   'Twas purchased for a price like this—

45

For silver pieces and a kiss,
But Judas would not understand.

Thou with Thine own unstained hand
  Didst wash the feet and humbly teach
  That such a task becometh each;
But Judas would not understand.

"Watch thou and pray," was Thy command,
  Lest, thoughtless, the disciples fall
  Beneath the tempter's bitter thrall;
But Judas would not understand.

☩

LORD, TAKE AWAY MY EVIL,

AND FILL ME WITH THY GOOD

The Second Wednesday

Behold, the days come, saith the Lord, that I will make a new covenant with the house of Israel, and with the house of Judah.

As often as ye eat this bread and drink this cup, ye do show the Lord's death till He come.

Luke 22:15-21

(Matt. 26:26-29; Mark 14:22-25; I Cor. 11:23-25)

And He said unto them, With desire I have desired to eat this passover with you before I suffer: for I say unto you, I shall not eat it, until it be fulfilled in the Kingdom of God. And He received a cup, and when He had given thanks, He said, Take this, and divide it among yourselves: for I say unto you, I shall not drink from henceforth of the fruit of the vine, until the kingdom of God shall come.

And He took bread, and when He had given thanks, He brake it, and gave to them, saying, This is my body which is given for you: this do in remembrance of me. And the cup in like manner after supper, saying, This cup is the new covenant in my blood, even that which is poured out for you. But behold, the hand of him that betrayeth me is with me on the table.

I

Luke presents the Lord's Supper as the culmination and fulfilment of the passover, setting before us the very moment at which the Blessed Sacrament burst like a flower from the stem of the Old Testament feast. He gives in the opening verses a summary of the passover meal in its two principal parts: the eating of the paschal lamb—with the unleavened bread and bitter herbs—and the drinking of "the cup of blessing." Of both Jesus partook with the disciples, telling them that it was the last time. When He would again eat and drink with them it would be in the final fulfilment of the passover in heaven. Meanwhile, however, there was to be a fulfilment on earth, which was even now beginning. The passover, commemorating Israel's deliverance from bondage in Egypt, prefigured the redemption of mankind from sin and death. This redemption, begun with Jesus' birth and carried forward through His life, was about to be completed by His death. In the Passion of Jesus, therefore, the Old Testament type was fulfilled. This was in truth the Last Supper. The passover as an institution had come to an end, just as the passover meal in the upper room had come to an end. The paschal lamb had been consumed; on the table were left only the fragments of the bread and the remainder of the wine. Out of these relics of the old feast Jesus now fashioned a new and more glorious feast. The passover bread was once more taken and consecrated and broken and given to the disciples. It was no longer "the bread of affliction" which their fathers had eaten in Egypt; it was Jesus' Body, which was being given for them. The passover cup, blessed before, was blessed anew and handed round. It was no longer the covenant made with

Moses; it was the new covenant, ratified by Jesus' Blood, which was being poured out for them. Thus the passover passed over into the Lord's Supper, as Richard Crashaw quaintly sings—

> Lo, the new Law of the new Lord
> With a new Lamb blesses the Board.
> The aged Pascha pleads not years,
> But spies love's dawn, and disappears.
> Types yield to Truths, shades shrink away,
> And their Night dies into our Day.

Jesus charged His disciples to continue keeping this feast, in order to perpetuate His memory and to hold fast and hand down for all time the meaning of His death. This was to be henceforth the covenant feast of God's people.

II

"Behold, the hand of him that betrayeth me is with me on the table." O boundless and indomitable Grace! In the night of blackest sin and guilt, Jesus, Thy love put forth its perfect flower. When men did their worst to Thee Thou hadst for them Thy best. O Love unto the uttermost! O Grace, where sin abounded, much more abounding! What wilt Thou refuse me, who hast given Thyself for me? What wilt Thou withhold from me, who dost give Thyself to me? Not only didst Thou offer up Thy holy Body and shed Thy most precious Blood for me on Calvary, but Thou givest me this Body to eat and this Blood to drink in the Holy Supper. Good Shepherd, who callest Thine own by name, Thou dost not only gladden me with Thy word of Absolution, saying most sweetly, "Son, be of good cheer: thy sins be forgiven"; but Thou dost seal, Thou dost certify to me this word by the visible sign and pledge of Thy Blessed Sacrament. Lo! Thou hast brought me to the banqueting house, and Thy banner over me is love. Thou givest us bread from heaven, and man doth eat Angels' food. Here is Bread, which if a man eat, he shall not die; here is Wine that maketh glad the heart of man. Hail, most Holy Body of Christ! Hail, Heavenly Drink of Jesus' Blood! to me above all things the sum of delight! It is for me; who else then should receive it but I—eagerly, humbly, frequently, worthily! O Lord, I am not worthy so much as to gather up the crumbs under Thy Table. Yet who is truly worthy and well prepared but he that believes these words, "Given and shed for you for the remission of sins"? Lord, I believe: help Thou mine unbelief. I am not worthy that Thou shouldst come under my roof; but speak the word only, and my soul shall be healed. In the multitude of Thy mercy I will come unto Thine Altar: O save and deliver me for Thy tender mercies' sake. O God, Thou art my God: my soul thirsteth for Thee, my flesh also longeth for Thee. Blessed is He, that cometh in the Name of the Lord: Hosanna in the highest. I have found Him whom my soul loveth; I will hold Him and not let Him go. My Beloved is mine, and I am His. How shall I thank Thee, O my sweet Redeemer, that Thou so lovest me as to come down to visit me? May Thy holy Body and Thy Precious Blood be to me meat and drink unto life eternal, that I may live in Thee and

Thou in me, until with Angels and Archangels, and with all the company of heaven, I shall perfectly laud and magnify Thy glorious Name, O Lord, Holy Father, Almighty Everlasting God, and praise Thee evermore. Maran atha: O our Lord, come!

III

LITANY OF THE HOLY COMMUNION

Lord, have mercy upon us,
Christ, have mercy upon us.
Lord, have mercy upon us,

O God the Father, Creator of the world,
O God the Son, Redeemer of mankind,
O God the Holy Ghost, Sanctifier of the Church,

Have mercy upon us, and fit us, unworthy sinners, to receive Thee.

Jesus, our Lord and God, Who vouchsafest to be present in the Holy Communion,

Jesus, our Heavenly Physician, Who givest Thyself to us to heal and comfort us,

Jesus, our gracious God, Who givest Thyself to us in the Holy Communion under the Bread and Wine,

Jesus, the Bread of Life, Which whosoever eateth, shall live for ever,

Jesus, the Good Shepherd, Who didst lay down Thy life for Thy sheep, and feedest them with Thine own Body and Blood,

Jesus, Who in this wonderful Sacrament art Thyself both Sacrifice and Priest,

Jesus, our adorable High Priest, Who ever livest to make intercession for us,

Have mercy upon us, and fit us, unworthy sinners, to receive Thee.

Have mercy, O Lord, and pardon our sins.
Have mercy, O Lord, and hear our prayers.

From unbelief in this Holy Sacrament,
From all irreverence during this awful service,
From neglecting to come, and from coming negligently,
From unworthy receiving of this Holy Sacrament,
From hardness of heart and ingratitude for so unspeakable
    a blessing.
By Thine Almighty Power, which orders all things as Thou
    pleasest,
By Thine Infinite Goodness in giving Thyself to us in this
    wonderful Mystery,
By Thy Blessed Body broken for us on the Cross, and really
    given to us in the Holy Communion,
By Thy Precious Blood shed for us on the Cross, and really
    given to us in the Cup of Blessing,
    Deliver us sinners, good Lord.
    We sinners beseech Thee to hear us.

That we may ever believe all Thy words teach us,
That before we approach this Holy Sacrament we may be
    reconciled to Thee, and be in perfect charity with all men,
That returning from this Sacrament we may praise and bless
    Thee, and strive diligently to amend our lives,
That by this heavenly medicine we may be healed and strength-
    ened against future falls,
That by this Holy Communion our hearts may be kindled
    to love Thee ever more and more,
That as we see Thee now by faith, under these visible forms,
    so we may hereafter see Thee face to face, and eternally
    enjoy Thy Presence,
    We beseech Thee to hear us, Good Lord.

O Lamb of God, That takest away the sin of the world,
    Spare us, O Lord.
O Lamb of God, That takest away the sin of the world,
    Have mercy upon us.

52

O Lamb of God, That takest away the sin of the world,
   Grant us Thy peace.

OUR FATHER.

   Lord, hear my prayer,
   And let my cry come unto Thee.

O LORD GOD, Who hast left unto us in a wonderful Sacrament a memorial of Thy Passion: Grant, we beseech Thee, that we may so use this Sacrament of Thy Body and Blood, that the fruits of Thy redemption may continually be manifest in us; Who livest and reignest with the Father and the Holy Ghost, ever One God, world without end. *Amen.*

IV

"PANGE LINGUA GLORIOSI"

Now, my tongue, the mystery telling
   Of the glorious Body sing,
And the Blood, all price excelling,
   Which the Gentiles' Lord and King,
In a Virgin's womb once dwelling,
   Shed for this world's ransoming.

Given for us, and condescending
   To be born for us below,
He with men in converse blending
   Dwelt the seed of truth to sow,
Till He closed with wondrous ending
   His most patient life of woe.

That last night at supper lying,
   'Mid the Twelve, His chosen band,
Jesus, with the law complying,
   Keeps the Feast its rites demand;

Then more precious Food supplying,
  Gives Himself with His own hand,

Word-made-Flesh, true bread He maketh
  By His Word His Flesh to be;
Wine, His Blood; which whoso taketh
  Must from carnal thoughts be free;
Faith alone, though sight forsaketh,
  Shows true hearts the Mystery.

Therefore we, before Him bending,
  This great Sacrament revere;
Types and shadows have their ending,
  For the newer Rite is here;
Faith, our outward sense befriending,
  Makes the inward vision clear.

✠

COME, LORD JESUS

The Second Thursday

Intreat me not to leave thee; or to return from following after thee.
For whither thou goest, I will go: and where thou lodgest, I will lodge.
Thy people shall be my people: and thy God my God.

John 14:1-6, 27; 15:1-2, 4-6

Let not your heart be troubled: believe in God, believe also in me. In my Father's house are many mansions; if it were not so, I would have told you; for I go to prepare a place for you. And if I go and prepare a place for you, I come again, and will receive you unto myself; that where I am, there ye may be also. And whither I go, ye know the way. Thomas saith unto Him, Lord, we know not whither Thou goest; how know we the way? Jesus saith unto him, I am the way, and the truth, and the life; no one cometh unto the Father, but by me.

Peace I leave with you; my peace I give unto you: not as the world giveth, give I unto you. Let not your heart be troubled, neither let it be fearful.

I am the true vine, and my Father is the husbandman. Every branch in me that beareth not fruit, He taketh it away: and every branch that beareth fruit, He cleanseth it, that it may bear more fruit. Abide in me, and I in you. As the branch cannot bear fruit of itself, except it abide in the vine; so neither can ye, except ye abide in me. I am the vine, ye are the branches: He that abideth in me, and I in him, the same beareth much fruit: for apart from me ye can do nothing. If a man abide not in me, he is cast forth as a branch, and is withered; and they gather them, and cast them into the fire, and they are burned.

I

In a long farewell discourse, spoken in the upper room and on the way to Gethsemane, Jesus forgetting His own sorrow set Himself to cheer the troubled hearts of His disciples. He was leaving them behind, strangers and pilgrims, like Himself, on the earth. But let them not be afraid. As a place had been found for Him, so one would be found also for them. What a fine large room their host had provided! So, in His Father's house were many mansions. How admirably Peter and John had made all things ready for this evening's meal! So He would prepare a place for them, an upper room of His own, furnished and ready in heaven. They should see how homelike everything would be. And then He would come to them, and they should be together again for ever. They had no need, therefore, to be troubled or fearful. Let them believe in God; He was the goal of their way: let them believe in Jesus; He was the way to their goal, a real and living way.

Voices were heard in the street below; friends were parting and bidding one another good night. "Peace be unto you"—thus the salutations rose to the disciples' ears. And He told them that He, too, was bidding His friends farewell. But His "Peace be unto you" was more than a conventional greeting. On the lips of others it was a mere wish, but when He said "Peace" He gave His peace into their hearts, so that they might never be disturbed. It was the peace that filled His own heart, and peace He had come to bring, the peace He was going by His death and resurrection to obtain for them, the peace of God that passeth all understanding.

The closing hymn was sung, and the little company passed from the lighted room, down the outer stairway, into the midnight street. Their way led past gardens in which vine-dressers had been at their springtime work, and from which came the odor of trimmed vines. He told His companions that He was the true Vine and that they were the branches. Only by abiding in Him, and having His life in them, could they bear fruit. In one place they were obliged to step over a heap of cuttings flung into the road, and He reminded them that in like manner dry branches would be cut off and living branches pruned by the heavenly Husbandman.

Of many other things He discoursed that night—of love and lasting joy, of persecution bravely to be met, of prayer in His name that would obtain whatever it asked, of the Comforter who would never leave them. Still other things He could not tell them, for they were unable as yet to bear them. The Spirit of truth, whom He was going to send, would lead them into all the truth.

II

Precious beyond all telling, my ever-present Lord, are these parting words of Thine. Though they were spoken on the eve of Thy death, there is upon them the light of Easter and of Pentecost. Thy going away, was it not in very truth Thy coming again? As Thou partest from Thy disciples, Thou dost call back over Thy shoulder, "I am coming to you." Thou comest in the coming of the Holy Ghost, that other Comforter who will abide with us for ever. He does not speak of Himself but testifies of Thee. He takes of Thine and shows it unto us. Therefore His coming is Thy coming, and in His abiding presence Thou art with us alway, even unto the end of the world. Let me not, my sweet Saviour, think of Thy cross apart from Thy crown; let me never hear or read Thy farewell sayings without feeling Thy presence by my side.

O Holy Spirit, most precious Fruit of Jesus' Passion, best Gift of my Redeemer, and Earnest of eternal blessedness!

> Come, Consoler, kindest, best,
> Come, our bosom's dearest Guest,
> Sweet refreshment, sweet repose.

Come! for I cannot by my own reason or strength believe in Jesus Christ my Lord, or come to Him. O Thou without whom no man can say that Jesus is Lord! come to me, in order that I may come to Him, without whom no man cometh unto the Father. Thou Promise of the Father, O most blessed Light! Thou hast called me through the Gospel, enlightened me with Thy seven-fold gifts, and sanctified and preserved me in true faith. Even so, Thou who art the One Spirit in the one mystical Body of Christ, dost call, gather, enlighten, and sanctify the whole Christian Church on earth, and preserve it in union with Jesus Christ in true faith. In this Christian Church, Thou Cleanser from sin, Thou Healer of wounds, dost daily forgive abundantly all my sins and the sins of all believers. O Spirit of Him that raised up Jesus from the dead, I believe that at the last day Thou wilt raise up me and all the dead, and wilt grant everlasting life to me and to all who believe in Christ. Spirit of truth, evermore keep us in this truth.

III

LITANY OF THE HOLY GHOST

> Lord, have mercy.
> Christ, have mercy.
> Lord, have mercy.

O God the Father in Heaven,
O God the Son, Redeemer of the world,
O God the Holy Ghost, the Comforter,
Holy Trinity, One God,
> Have mercy upon us.

Holy Spirit, Author of all good,
Holy Spirit, Who didst overshadow the blessed Virgin Mary,
Holy Spirit, Who didst descend upon Christ in the form of a dove,
Holy Spirit, Who on the Day of Pentecost didst appear in fiery tongues upon the disciples,
> Have mercy upon us.

Spirit of Wisdom and Understanding,
Spirit of Counsel and Might,
Spirit of Knowledge and Piety,
Spirit of the Fear of the Lord,
Spirit of holy Repentance,

Spirit of Grace and Prayer,
Spirit of Love, Peace and Joy,
Spirit of Gentleness, Goodness and Faith,
Spirit of manifold Grace,
  Have mercy upon us.

Spirit of Truth, Who guidest us into all truth,
Spirit Who helpest our infirmities,
Spirit Who sheddest the Love of God in our hearts,
Holy Spirit, by Whom we are born again,
Holy Spirit, Who dwellest in us,
Holy Spirit, Who abidest with us for ever,
Holy Ghost the Comforter,
Holy Ghost the Sanctifier,
  Have mercy upon us.

From all evil,
From the snares of the devil,
From presumption and despair,
From doubting and unbelief,
From envy and unkindness,
From obstinacy and impenitence,
From anger and strife,
From all unholiness and impurity,
From dulness and sloth,
From every evil spirit,
  Deliver us, O Holy Spirit.

That Thou wouldest reprove the world of sin, of righteous-
    ness, and of judgment,
That Thou wouldest glorify Christ to us and through us,
That Thou wouldest help us to love one another,
That Thou wouldest teach us to pray, and Thyself pray with-
    in us,
That Thou wouldest inspire us with holy thoughts, and a
    hatred of sin,
That Thou wouldest help us to remember that our body is
    Thy temple,

That Thou wouldest endue us with the grace of perseverance,
Holy Ghost, we beseech Thee to hear us.

O Lamb of God, That takest away the sin of the world,
Grant us Thy Holy Spirit.
O Lamb of God, That takest away the sin of the world,
Pour down upon us Thy Holy Spirit.
O Lamb of God, That takest away the sin of the world,
Give unto us the Spirit of Peace.
OUR FATHER.

For Guidance on the Way

JESUS OUR MASTER, do Thou meet us while we
walk in the way, and long to reach the Country; so
that following Thy light, we may keep the way of
righteousness, and never wander away into the hor-
rible darkness of this world's night, while Thou, Who
art the Way, the Truth, and the Life, art shining within us. *Amen.*

IV

"OUR BLEST REDEEMER, ERE HE BREATHED"

Our blest Redeemer, ere He breathed
  His tender last farewell,
A Guide, a Comforter bequeathed
  With us to dwell.

He came sweet influence to impart,
  A gracious, willing Guest,
While He can find one humble heart
  Wherein to rest.

And His that gentle voice we hear,
  Soft as the breath of even,

61

That checks each thought, that calms each fear,
  And speaks of heaven.

And every virtue we possess,
  And every victory won,
And every thought of holiness,
  Is His alone.

Spirit of purity and grace,
  Our weakness, pitying, see;
O make our hearts Thy dwelling-place,
  And worthier Thee.

☩

MAY THE GRACE OF THE HOLY SPIRIT ILLUMINE
MY HEART AND MIND

The Second Friday

9. THE HIGH PRIEST'S PRAYER

---

*The Lord hath sworn, and will not repent: Thou art
a priest for ever, after the order of Melchizedek.*

*Wherefore He is able to save them to the uttermost
that come unto God by Him: seeing He ever liveth to
make intercession for them.*

John 17:1, 4-5, 11, 15, 17, 20-21, 24-26

Father, the hour is come; glorify Thy Son, that the
Son may glorify Thee. I glorified Thee on the earth,
having accomplished the work which Thou hast given
me to do. And now, Father, glorify Thou me with
Thine own self with the glory which I had with Thee
before the world was.

Holy Father, keep them in Thy name which Thou
hast given me, that they may be one, even as we are.
I pray not that Thou shouldest take them from the
world, but that Thou shouldest keep them from the
evil one. Sanctify them in the truth: Thy word is
truth.

Neither for these only do I pray, but for them also
that believe on me through their word; that they may
all be one; even as Thou, Father, art in me, and I in
Thee, that they also may be in us: that the world may
believe that Thou didst send me.

Father, I desire that they also whom Thou hast
given me be with me where I am, that they may behold my glory, which Thou hast given me: for Thou
lovedst me before the foundation of the world.

O righteous Father, the world knew Thee not, but
I knew Thee; and these knew that Thou didst send
me; and I made known unto them Thy name, and

will make it known; that the love wherewith Thou
lovedst me may be in them, and I in them.

I

Before crossing the brook Kidron and entering the
dark garden, Jesus, with His disciples about Him, offered up His High-priestly Prayer.

He exulted that now at last the hour had come in
which He was to suffer and enter into His glory. All
His life had been devoted to glorifying the Father, re-
vealing Him as God who so loved the world that He
gave His Only-begotten Son, that whosoever believeth
in Him should not perish, but have everlasting life.
Now He prayed the Father to glorify Him in His
death, to declare Him to be indeed the Only-begotten
from the Father full of grace and truth.

His thoughts turned to the eleven men by His side,
through whose ministry this love and grace and truth
were to be brought to men. For their safety and sanctity He prayed—that the Father would keep them from
the evil one, in whose power the whole world lies, and
make them holy through His word and truth, so that
their preaching might be reinforced by their life. O
that He would make them one in the unity of the
same holy purpose that made Jesus and His Father
one!

His heart glowed as He thought of the many who
would believe through their word, which is God's
word—those other sheep of His, that would hear His
voice and would form with His first followers one

flock under one Shepherd; and He put out His arms and took them into His prayer.

His intercession gathered force and fervor as it neared its close. The deepest longing of His soul burst forth in an importunate "Father, I will!" His heart's desire was that all those who were the Father's gift to Him might be with Him and might behold His glory, which was the Father's gift to Him. The two gifts belonged together, and were in reality one. He asked it for the sake of the eternal love the Father had for Him.

Not only to the Father's love did He appeal, but to His justice. Shall not the Judge of all the earth do right? In the spirit of Abraham pleading for Sodom He called the Father to witness that though the world did not know Him, yet He, Jesus, knew Him and had made Him known to the disciples. Here was the little company of righteous in the midst of a wicked world, for whose sake God might well spare mankind. And this little company would grow into a multitude that no man could number; for Jesus pledged Himself to continue making the Father ever better known to them —through the Spirit whom He would send, and who would abide with them for ever and guide them into all truth—so that the love of God resting upon Jesus, and Jesus Himself as bearer of this love, might become a living and saving reality in their midst.

II

O Jesus, interceding for Thine own! I am filled with wonder and with awe as I contemplate Thee pouring

out Thy heart in prayer. All Thy life on earth was a
life of prayer; truly, Thou didst pray without ceasing.
I see Thee at Thy mother's knee learning Thy childish
devotions, and in the synagogue joining in the common worship of the Church. I behold Thee praying
at the Baptism in Jordan; in a solitary place near
Capernaum a great while before dawn; before choosing the Twelve; after the return of the Seventy; at
Thy Transfiguration; before giving Thy disciples the
"Our Father"; at the grave of Lazarus. But in the time
of Thy Passion, O my Lord, Thy prayers become more
frequent and more fervent; they rise from lower depths
and soar to loftier heights. I adore Thee for Thy pleading for foolish Peter, Thy High-priestly Intercession,
Thy Agony in the garden, Thy prayers upon the
Cross. Here Thou art most completely at one with the
deepest need and longing of man and with the holy
and loving will of God. In the prayers of the Passion
I behold Thee as indeed the one Mediator between
God and man. And looking up to heaven, I see Thee
now, at the right hand of God, ever living to make intercession for us. Thou art the same there as here. O
High Priest of good things to come, in Thy prayer at
the threshold of the Passion Thou hast given us a
precious summary of the intercession Thou now makest for us in glory. Ever pray for us, Jesus our Ad-
vocate with the Father.

Like the disciples of old I see Thee praying, and I
cry, "Lord, teach me to pray!" Teach me to pray like
Thee: in Thy spirit, childlike, confident, obedient,
coming to God as to my Father, with all cheerfulness

and boldness, knowing that He heareth me always; saying in all that pertains to His name, His kingdom, and His will, "Father, I will!"; in all that pertains to myself, "Not my will, but Thine be done." Teach me to pray through Thee: in Thy Name and for Thy sake, in complete dependence on Thy merit, and with perfect faith in Thy word, "The Father Himself loveth you, because ye have loved me, and have believed that I came out from God." Teach me to pray to Thee, who having glorified the Father on the earth, hast been glorified by Him with the glory that Thou hadst with Him before the foundation of the world. Hast not Thou said, "If we ask any thing in My Name, I will do it"? Alas! I know not how to pray as I ought. Grant me, therefore, Thy Spirit to help my infirmities and to make intercession for me and in me. And whenever I lift my heart to Thee, may Thy all prevailing prayer take my poor stumbling prayer by the hand, and as an elder brother lead it to the throne of grace. So shall it be heard and answered exceeding abundantly above all that I ask or think.

III

"Prayer Shall Be Made for Him Continually"

Almighty and Everlasting God, at Whose right hand Thy Son, our Saviour and High Priest Jesus Christ, maketh intercession for us: Give ear, we beseech Thee, to His prayer, and grant Him His heart's desire, that we may be with Him where He is, to behold His glory, which Thou hast given Him; through the same Jesus Christ our Lord. *Amen.*

For Boldness in Prayer

Our great high priest, Who art passed into the heavens, Jesus the Son of God, Who didst offer Thyself, and ever livest to make intercession for us: Grant unto us, Thine unworthy servants, boldness to enter into the holiest by Thy Blood, that we may obtain mercy and find grace to help in time of need; O Thou Who art able to save us to the uttermost. *Amen.*

For Help to Pray in Jesus' Name

Lord God the Holy Ghost, Spirit of Grace and Prayer, Who makest intercession for them that know not how to pray: We entreat Thee to help our infirmities, so that we, uniting our prayers to those of our High Priest, and asking in human weakness the things for which He pleads in heavenly glory, may truly pray in Jesus' Name, and obtain whatever we ask; through the same Jesus Christ our Lord, Who liveth and reigneth with the Father and with Thee, One God, blessed for ever. *Amen.*

IV

THE MEDIATOR

Where high the heavenly temple stands,
The house of God not made with hands,
A great High Priest our nature wears,
The Saviour of mankind appears.

THE HIGH PRIEST'S PRAYER

He Who for men their surety stood,
And poured on earth His precious Blood,
Pursues in heaven His mighty plan,
The Saviour and the Friend of man.

Though now ascended up on high,
He bends on earth a Brother's eye;
Partaker of the human name,
He knows the frailty of our frame.

In every pang that rends the heart
The Man of Sorrows had a part,
He sympathizes in our grief,
And to the sufferer sends relief.

With boldness, therefore, at the throne
Let us make all our sorrows known,
And ask the aid of heavenly power,
To help us in the evil hour.

☩

PRAY FOR ME, LORD JESUS, AND TEACH ME TO PRAY

The Second Saturday

10. THE AGONY IN THE GARDEN

The sorrows of death compassed me, and the pains
of hell gat hold upon me: I found trouble and sorrow.
Then called I upon the name of the Lord: O Lord,
I beseech Thee, deliver my soul.

Matthew 26:36-46

(Mark 14:32-42; Luke 22:39-46).

Then cometh Jesus with them unto a place called
Gethsemane, and saith unto His disciples, Sit ye here,
while I go yonder and pray. And He took with Him
Peter and the two sons of Zebedee, and began to be
sorrowful and sore troubled. Then saith He unto
them, My soul is exceeding sorrowful, even unto
death: abide ye here, and watch with me. And He
went forward a little, and fell on His face, and prayed,
saying, My Father, if it be possible, let this cup pass
away from me: nevertheless, not as I will, but as
Thou Wilt. And He cometh unto the disciples, and
findeth them sleeping, and saith unto Peter, What,
could ye not watch with me one hour? Watch and
pray, that ye enter not into temptation: the spirit
indeed is willing, but the flesh is weak. Again a second time He went away, and prayed, saying, My Father, if this cannot pass away, except I drink it, Thy
will be done. And He came again and found them
sleeping, for their eyes were heavy. And He left them
again, and went away, and prayed a third time, saying
again the same words. Then cometh He to the disciples, and sayeth again unto them, Sleep on now,
and take your rest: Behold, the hour is at hand, and

the Son of Man is betrayed into the hands of sinners. Arise, let us be going: behold, he is at hand that betrayeth me.

I

Matthew gives the fullest account of the Agony in Gethsemane and shows most clearly the progress of Jesus' struggle, from prayer to prayer, to perfect peace. "O my Father!"—so he began, with the invariable address of the well-beloved Son. But a few hours before, He had given His disciples the cup of blessing in the Holy Supper, pouring into it His grace and truth, His love and life. Now His suffering presented itself to Him under the same figure of a cup—a cup of trembling and of fury, in which were mingled the sin and falsity, the hatred and treachery of men. And He cried, "Let this cup pass from me!" He said, "If it is possible," not "if it be possible." He believed, therefore, that He might not need to drink it; in Mark His words are, "Abba, Father, all things are possible unto Thee." He reckoned with the possibility of divine intervention, not to save Himself the pain, but His people the sin. On this condition alone did He permit Himself to pray for the passing of the cup. But no sooner were the words out of His mouth than He seemed to clutch for them as if to take them back, and hastened to add, "Nevertheless, not as I will, but as Thou wilt."

He returned to find His three friends asleep. With loving irony He reminded them, through their spokesman Peter, of their promise to die with Him, and bade them watch and pray. The spirit was eager enough, but the flesh—ah, did not He know it?—was weak.

He left them and resumed His prayer. In the altered form of the second prayer may be seen the answer to the first. "O my Father," He said, "if it is not possible for this cup to pass without my drinking it, Thy will be done." It had become clear to Him that the cup could not pass from Him, that this acceptance was the only way. Hence He no longer mentioned His own will; He did not even pray that His will be not done, so completely was it lost in the Father's will. He said simply the third petition of the prayer He had taught His disciples—laconic, all-inclusive, final.

Again He returned to the sleepers, but did not disturb them. He went away and prayed the third time, using the same words, "Thy will be done." It was no vain repetition, but the completion and confirmation of the victory already won. Then back to the three disciples with words pitying yet stern, "Still sleeping? Resting so soundly? Poor children, you must arise now; the hour is come, and with it my betrayer."

II

What was it, good Jesus, that caused Thee to be greatly amazed and sore troubled? Surely, Thou didst not shrink from death! What terrors, indeed, could death have had for Thee? The sting of death is sin, and Thou knewest no sin. But God made Thee to be sin for us; the Lord laid on Thee the iniquity of us all.

Thou hadst done no violence, neither was any deceit in Thy mouth; yet Thou wast wounded for our transgressions, Thou wast bruised for our iniquities. Thou wast the Lamb of God, taking away the sin of the world. Ah, and there was in Thy cup an even bitterer drop. Thou couldst take away the sin of the world only by means of Thy people's sin. Thou couldst die for all men only by dying at the hands of thy countrymen. The treason of Judas, the hatred and injustice of the priests, the rejection by the people of their Messiah —these broke Thy heart. Thus did sin beset Thee behind and before. From this Thy pure soul shrank with loathing unutterable. This caused Thee to be exceeding sorrowful even unto death, and to plead for another way, if one might be found; this drew from Thee Thy strong crying and tears and bloody sweat. O my Lord, my Lord, how foul and fearsome a thing is sin, the sin I lightly commit every day! Ever when tempted, let me see Thee on Thy face in the dust of the garden, broken-hearted, compassed with the sorrows of death, the pains of hell. Open mine eyes to the exceeding sinfulness of sin; teach me to hate it with Thy perfect hatred.

Thy prayers in the garden were heard and answered, O Lord, my Lord. Thou wast heard because of Thy godly fear. Did not Thy Father hear Thee always? If the prayer of a righteous man availeth much in its working, how much more Thy prayer, Thou Righteous Servant of the Lord! I can trace the answer in the progress of the prayers themselves, in the tranquil majesty with which Thou wentest to meet Thy cap-

tors, in Thy patience at the trial, in Thy obedience
unto death, in Thy exaltation on the third day. Thy
word on the Cross, "It is finished," was it not a cry of
gratitude to the Father for having heard Thy prayers?
Then was Thy soul satisfied, Thy joy fulfilled. O say
to us, over and over again, as Thou saidst to Thy disciples, "Ask, and ye shall receive, that your joy may
be full."

III

For the Merit of Christ's Agony

LORD JESUS CHRIST, Whose sweat became for my
sake as great drops of blood falling to the ground, succor me, I pray Thee, in the sweat and agony of my
last hour. O Thou Who didst endure for us the wrath
of God, deliver us from the wrath to come. Grant me
to watch and pray, that I may not enter into temptation. *Amen.*

For Conformity to God's Will

GOD ALMIGHTY, Eternal, Righteous, and Merciful, give to us poor sinners to do for Thy sake all that
we know of Thy will, and to will always what pleases
Thee, so that inwardly purified, enlightened, and kindled by the fire of the Holy Spirit, we may follow in
the footprints of Thy Well-Beloved Son, our Lord Jesus Christ. *Amen.*

"Thy Will Be Done"

O GOD, THE FATHER IN HEAVEN, Whose gracious
and good will is done without our prayer, we pray

Thee that it may be done by us also. To this end do
Thou bring to naught the will of the devil, the world,
and our own flesh, which would prevent the hallowing
of Thy Name and the coming of Thy Kingdom; and
strengthen and keep us steadfast in Thy Word and
in true faith even unto our end; through Jesus Christ
Thy Son our Lord. *Amen*.

IV

"O SOUL OF JESUS, SICK TO DEATH"

O soul of Jesus, sick to death!
   Thy Blood and prayer together plead;
My sins have bowed Thee to the ground,
   As the storm bows the feeble reed.

My God! My God! and can it be
   That I should sin so lightly now,
And think no more of evil thoughts
   Than of the wind that waves the bough?

Shall it be always thus, O Lord?
   Wilt Thou not work this hour in me
The grace Thy Passion merited,
   Hatred of self and love of Thee?

Oh, by the pains of Thy pure love,
   Grant me the gift of holy fear:
And give me of Thy Bloody Sweat
   To wash my guilty conscience clear!

Ever when tempted, make me see,
   Beneath the olive's moon-pierced shade,
My God, alone, outstretched, and bruised,
   And bleeding, on the earth He made.

THE MAN OF SORROWS

And make me feel it was my sin,
   As though no other sins there were,
That was to Him who bears the world,
   A load that He could scarcely bear!

☩

MY FATHER, MAKE ME DEEPLY LOVE THEE, AND ALL
THOU WILLEST FOR ME

The Second Monday

Then said I, Lo, I come: in the volume of the book
it is written of me.
  I delight to do Thy will, O my God: yea, Thy law
is within my heart.

John 18:1-9

When Jesus had spoken these words, He went forth
with His disciples over the brook Kidron, where was
a garden, into which He entered, Himself and His
disciples. Now Judas also, who betrayed Him, knew
the place: for Jesus ofttimes resorted thither with His
disciples. Judas then, having received the band of soldiers, and officers from the chief priests and the Pharisees, cometh thither with lanterns and torches and
weapons. Jesus therefore, knowing all the things that
were coming upon Him, went forth, and saith unto
them, Whom seek ye? They answered Him, Jesus of
Nazareth. Jesus saith unto them, I am He. And Judas
also, who betrayed Him, was standing with them.
When therefore He said unto them, I am He, they
went backward, and fell to the ground. Again therefore He asked them, Whom seek ye? And they said,
Jesus of Nazareth. Jesus answered, I told you that I
am He; if therefore ye seek me, let these go their
way: that the word might be fulfilled which He spake,
Of those whom Thou hast given me I lost not one.

I

While the Master was rousing His disciples there
sounded the tramp of soldiers, and between the tree-

trunks appeared the flash of lanterns and the glint of arms. Though they had the traitor with them, they came prepared for resistance or at least flight. There is a touch of irony in the scene—instead of fleeing or hiding behind the trees of the garden, Jesus came openly toward them and asked, "Whom seek ye?" Instead of offering resistance He said, "I am He."

This was so unexpected a turn of events that the men were completely taken aback; they recoiled and fell to the earth. The lights wavered, the weapons clattered to the ground. As the eyes of a fearless man will hold in leash a pack of wild beasts, so the holy God-Man by His mere presence overpowered this band of wicked men. The gleam of majesty on His face and ring of authority in His voice they could not endure. While they lay helpless, how easily He might have escaped! But that was not His purpose; what He had in mind was to set forth the truth of His saying, "Therefore doth my Father love me, because I lay down my life, that I may take it again. No man taketh it from me, but I lay it down of myself. I have power to lay it down, and I have power to take it again."

These men would not have been so surprised if they had seen Him on His knees in the garden, and if they had understood how in prayer He won His way to the center of the Father's will. They would have recognized the result and answer of that prayer in His attitude toward them, and they would have heard in His "I am He" the echo of His "Here am I" to the Father in heaven. That is why John says that "knowing all the things that were coming upon Him," Jesus went forth to meet the armed band.

With His enemies prone before Him, Jesus was in a position to dictate terms and to demand the safety of His followers. If it was He the soldiers were seeking, let them take Him and do to Him whatever they pleased, or rather whatever God pleased; but let them spare His disciples. The escape of the company of disciples was the result not only of their own cowardice and flight, but of their Lord's offering Himself in their behalf. He put Himself as a wall of defence between them and the foe. In their immunity John finds the deeper fulfilment of Jesus' words in the High-priestly Prayer, "Of those whom Thou hast given me I lost not one."

II

"Whom seek ye?" It is as though He could not wait until they led Him away to suffer; He must needs run before and meet them in the way, lest they should not find Him, or take some other in His stead. Like David, He hasted and ran to meet the foe. So impatient to suffer for me was the All-Patient One. John Bunyan, in his "Holy War," pictures the King calling his Son and bidding Him go forth to capture the town of Mansoul. "Then said the King's Son, 'Thy law is within my heart! I delight to do Thy will. This is the day that I have longed for, and the work that I have waited for all this while. My heart has been often pained within me for the miserable town of Mansoul; but now it is rejoiced, but now it is glad.' And with that he leaped for joy, saying, 'The day of vengeance is in mine heart for thee, my Mansoul; and glad am I that Thou, my Father, hast made me the Captain of their salvation.'" Even so my Lord made haste to deliver me, my Strength to help me. As a bridegroom He came out of His chamber, and rejoiced as a strong man to run a race. He hastened to embrace the Cross for love of me, and in obedience to His Father's will He went to meet His captors while they were yet far off. A perfect obedience! O eager energy of love! Alas, how slow am I to obey, how ready to draw back from suffering. Good Jesus, give me the will to say, in face of every duty, every danger, "Here am I."

"Whom seek ye?" How many persons and things we seek beside Thee, O Thou that art fairer than the children of men! We seek our own pleasure and ease, our own gain, our own will and way. Yet, if we but knew, all the restless seeking and striving of our hearts is an unconscious reaching out and feeling after Thee, Thou Hidden Treasure, Thou Pearl of great price. Thou art the substance of all the shadows we pursue. Thou standest before us, hidden behind the wall, or showing Thy face but dimly through the lattice. In unexpected moments Thy voice falls on our ear, Thy figure startles and waylays. Concealed behind altars built to unknown gods; in heathen temples obscured by the smoke of strange offerings, Thou whisperest, "Whom seek ye? I am He." Thou goest forth to meet those that know Thee not, or that hate Thy name and wish Thee harm. Thou pursuest them that fly from Thee to wisdom and pleasure that are not Thine. And

when Thy footfall halts beside me, a "voice is round
me like a bursting sea"—

> Ah, fondest, blindest, weakest,
> I am He whom Thou seekest.
> Thou dravest love from thee, who dravest Me.

"Whom seek ye?" Jesus of Nazareth, my Lord and
my God! It is Thou I seek, and not another. Let me
find Thee. Find me, in order that I may find Thee.
Take me captive, in order that I may become Thy cap-
tor, one of faith's violent ones who take Thy kingdom
by force, who bind Thee with cords of love. I will not
let Thee go, except Thou bless me. Whom have I in
heaven but Thee? and there is none upon earth that I
desire beside Thee.

III

For Whole-Hearted Surrender

O LORD JESUS CHRIST, Who to atone for my disobedience didst yield Thyself into the hands of Thine
enemies, grant that I may willingly and with my
whole heart yield myself up to Thee, and live, suffer,
and die according to Thy will. *Amen.*

For Courage

O LORD, Who when Thine hour was come didst
go without fear among those that sought Thy life:
Give me, I pray Thee, such boldness to confess Thee
before men, and such readiness to bear the cross, that
hereafter Thou mayest confess me before Thy Father
Who is in heaven, and give me to inherit an eternal

crown; for Thine own merit's sake, our Lord and Saviour. *Amen.*

For the Safety of a True Disciple

Lord jesus christ, Who didst deliver up Thyself to those who came to take Thee captive, and didst
plead for Thy disciples, saying, "If ye seek me, let these
go their way": Make me to be numbered with Thy
true disciples, that so Thy Passion and Death may set
me free from the wrath of God and the fear of men.
Amen.

IV

CHRIST AND THE PAGAN

I had no God but these,
The sacerdotal Trees,
And they uplifted me.
"I hung upon a Tree."

The sun and moon I saw,
And reverential awe
Subdued me day and night.
"I am the perfect Light."

Within a lifeless Stone—
All other gods unknown—
I sought Divinity.
"The Corner-Stone am I."

For sacrificial feast
I slaughtered man and beast,
Red recompense to gain.
"So I, a Lamb, was slain.

82

"WHOM SEEK YE?"

"Yea; such My hungering Grace
That wheresoe'er My face
Is hidden, none may grope
Beyond eternal Hope."

✠

O JESUS, MAY MY LOVE TO THEE CAST OUT ALL FEAR

The Second Tuesday

12. THE KISS AND THE SWORD

---

*Faithful are the wounds of a friend; but the kisses of
an enemy are profuse.*
*Deliver my soul from the sword: my darling from
the power of the dog.*

Matthew 26:47-56

(Mark 14:43-49; Luke 22:47-53; John 18:10-11).

And while He yet spake, lo, Judas, one of the twelve,
came, and with him a great multitude with swords
and staves, from the chief priests and elders of the
people. Now he that betrayed Him gave them a sign,
saying, Whomsoever I shall kiss, that is He: take
Him. And straightway he came to Jesus, and said,
Hail, Rabbi; and kissed Him. And Jesus said unto
him, Friend, do that for which thou art come. Then
they came and laid hands on Jesus, and took Him.
And behold, one of them that were with Jesus
stretched out his hand, and drew his sword, and
smote the servant of the high priest, and struck off
his ear. Then saith Jesus unto him, Put up again thy
sword into its place: for all they that take the sword
shall perish with the sword. Or thinkest thou that I
cannot beseech my Father, and He shall even now
send me more than twelve legions of Angels? How
then should the Scriptures be fulfilled, that thus it
must be? In that hour said Jesus to the multitudes,
Are ye come out as against a robber with swords and
staves to seize me? I sat daily in the temple teaching, and ye took me not. But all this is come to pass,
that the scriptures of the prophets might be fulfilled.

I

The encounter with the soldiers made superfluous the sign of identification agreed upon between them and Judas; but, as persons guilty of great wrong are often most punctilious in the performance of minor duties, Judas felt bound to carry out the agreement to the letter. He now came up and greeted his Master in the customary manner, with "Hail, Rabbi," and the disciple's kiss. But because his greeting was not from the heart, he must needs kiss eagerly, effusively, again and again. So Joab said to Amasa, "Art thou in health, my brother?" and took him by the beard to kiss him, and drove his sword into his breast. Jesus' reply to Judas, which forms the dependent clause of a broken sentence, has been variously completed and explained. It seems best to leave it in its incomplete form, as the instinctive revulsion of a pure and loving nature, as instinctively repressed—"My man, that for which you are here. . . ."

Meanwhile the soldiers closed in on Jesus and arrested Him. At this point one of His companions sprang to His defence. John tells us that it was Peter, and we might have guessed as much. Peter had promised to follow his Lord to prison and to death; he was determined to keep his word despite, or rather, because of the fact that he had been unable to watch with Him during His agony. He drew a sword he had brought with him, and swung it for a mighty blow. Would that he might sever at one stroke the heads of all Jesus' foes! Alas! he succeeded only in flicking off

the ear of perhaps the humblest man present. It was
not only an empty flourish, but endangered the cause
it was intended to serve. Jesus bade His hasty disciple
return his sword to its sheath. How little He needed
Peter's aid! If it were a question of defence, His Father could send Him twelve legions and more of the
heavenly host, His angels that excel in strength. It was
not a question of defence, but of obedience. Hence
Jesus appealed to no sword either of men or of angels,
but to the written word and will of God; He faced
His enemies with the shining weapon of Truth. More
scathing words never fell from His lips; like a two-
edged sword they flashed in the darkness of the garden, piercing to the thoughts and intents of His captors' hearts, and laying bare their cowardice and hypocrisy. Their torches and swords and cudgels were not
only unnecessary, they were utterly impotent. For what
gave these men their power over Jesus was the truth of
the Scripture, which He was now fulfilling.

II

Let me beware of delivering my Lord to His enemies.
What a revolting scene—this kiss of betrayal! Here the
traitor completes his crime and seals his doom! it is
his farewell to life and love. Never was the sign and
pledge of love used for a baser purpose. Could he not
have spared his Master this last indignity? Better far,
to step up and strike Him in the face before them all!
That would have been an honest and consistent act at
least; it would have served equally well to identify
Jesus, and it would have been easier for Him to bear.

But hold, my soul—no stones! As I look upon this man in the garden, with the torchlight playing upon his face, do I find in him no resemblance to myself? Have I never, by hypocrisy in my devotions, by irreverence at service, by profanity in my intercourse with men or silence at the profanity of others, or by a life of open wickedness, delivered my Lord into the hands of His foes? Have I, while touching with my lips His Body and Blood in the Holy Sacrament, harbored evil and traitorous thoughts in my heart, and thus repeated the very kiss of Judas? O my Lord, forgive! O Lord, have mercy! O Lord, do not cast me off! I am no better than Judas, but do not cast me off! If Thou, Lord shouldest mark iniquities, O Lord, who shall stand?

Let me beware no less of wrongly defending my Lord against His enemies. Let me never seek to serve His cause with carnal weapons. How often have Christians been guilty of this folly and sin! They trust not the power of the Truth, and seek to reinforce it with the sword. How often has the Church usurped the function of the State and wielded the steel sword! All such attempts must fail, as Peter's failed. They bring boundless harm upon the cause of Christ, they endanger and retard His reign. Some have turned the Word itself into an earthly sword, and made of the Gospel a new law, of Christ a second Moses. They depend on laws and commands, on repression and compulsion, to bring about the regeneration of mankind. Let them put the sword back in its place and leave it where it belongs! By the sword men perish, but by the Word of truth they live and are made free. The Gospel alone is the power of God unto salvation to every one that believes. Give into my hand, good Jesus, this sword of the Spirit; then shall I be well armed against all foes without and within.

III

For Dependence on the Truth

LORD JESUS, Who wast wickedly betrayed and falsely defended by Thine Apostles, and bound and led away captive by Thine enemies: Give me grace that I may never pay Thee homage with lying lips, nor lose my trust in the power of Thine eternal Word, but confidently witness to Thy Truth before all men. Grant that Thy bonds may set me free from the bondage of sin and every evil. O Lord, in Thee have I trusted: let me never be confounded. *Amen.*

For the Church

GRANT, we beseech Thee, Almighty God, unto Thy Church, Thy Holy Spirit, and the wisdom that cometh down from above, that Thy Word, as becometh it, may not be bound, but have free course and be preached to the joy and edifying of Christ's holy people, that in steadfast faith we may serve Thee, and in the confession of Thy Name abide unto the end; through Jesus Christ Thy Son our Lord. *Amen.*

For Those in Authority

O MERCIFUL Father in heaven, Who holdest in Thy hand all the might of man, and Who hast or-

dained the powers that be for the punishment of evil-
doers and for the praise of them that do well, and of
Whom is all rule and authority in the kingdoms of
the world: We humbly beseech Thee, graciously regard
Thy servants, the President of the United States, the
Governor of this Commonwealth, our Judges and
Magistrates, and all the Rulers of the earth; that all
who receive the sword, as Thy ministers, may bear it
according to Thy commandment; through Jesus Christ
Thy Son our Lord. *Amen.*

IV

THE ARREST

"Arise! arise! they come!" Look how they run!
Alas, what haste they make to be undone!
How with their lanterns do they seek the Sun!
    Was ever grief like Mine?

With clubs and staves they seek Me as a thief,
Who am the way of truth, the true relief,
Most true to those who are my greatest grief:
    Was ever grief like Mine?

Judas, dost thou betray Me with a kiss?
Canst thou find hell about My lips, and miss
Of Life just at the gates of life and bliss?
    Was ever grief like Mine?

See, they lay hold on Me, not with the hands
Of faith, but fury; yet at their commands
I suffer binding, Who have loos'd their bands:
    Was ever grief like Mine?

THE MAN OF SORROWS

All my disciples flee; fear puts a bar
Betwixt My friends and Me; they leave the Star
That brought the wise men of the East from far:
    Was ever grief like Mine?

✠

GOOD JESUS, TAKE FROM ME ALL THAT IS NOT THINE
AND GIVE ME WHAT IS THINE

The Third Wednesday

13. FLIGHT

I was a reproach among all mine enemies: and a fear to mine acquaintance.
   They that did see me without fled from me.

Mark 14:50-52

(Matt. 26:56)

And they all left Him, and fled. And a certain young man followed with Him, having a linen cloth cast about him, over his naked body: and they lay hold on him; but he left the linen cloth, and fled naked.

I

In connection with the flight of the disciples Mark records a curious little incident, which has been called his artist's signature in a dark corner of his canvas. It is supposed that the young man referred to was the evangelist himself. There is indeed no point in the little night scene taken alone; it adds nothing to the history of the passion, and we should be none the poorer for its omission. It can be best accounted for on the supposition that Mark wished to paint his own portrait, in however unfavorable a light, into the Passion story, just as he had sketched into it the picture of his home.

There are good reasons for believing that it was an upper room in the house of Mark in which Jesus and

His disciples kept the Last Supper. Its location, on the outskirts of the city toward the Mount of Olives, has been identified with a considerable degree of probability. Afterwards this house of Mary, the mother of Mark, became a well known rendezvous for the Christians of Jerusalem. To it Peter naturally turned his steps after his release from Herod's prison. A humorous little tale connected with that midnight visit was current in the family, and found its way into the book of the Acts, where it stands as one of the many inimitable human elements in the Divine Word.

On that earlier midnight of our Lord's arrest, Mark, who had retired when Jesus and the eleven left the upper room, was awakened by the tramp of the soldiers past the house, on their way to Gethsemane. Rising from bed and not staying to dress, he hastened after them with only a linen sheet cast about his body. He may have witnessed the kiss of Judas and the flash of Peter's sword in the garden. He mingled with the crowd and went along with them for a time, after the disciples had disappeared. But when the soldiers spied him and laid hands on him, he was seized with terror, and slipping out of their grasp left the sheet behind and fled naked through the night.

If our reconstruction of the scene is correct this conduct is entirely in keeping with what we know of Mark's character. He did much the same thing when he accompanied Barnabas and Saul on their mission to Asia Minor—at Perga he left his companions and returned home. This caused a breach between the two missionaries, when Barnabas wished Mark to accompany them a second time and Paul refused to take along one who had not gone with them "to the work." It is pleasant to know that Paul afterwards changed his opinion of the young man, and in his last letter requested Timothy to bring Mark with him to Rome, "for he is useful to me for ministering." Who knows how large a part the memory of that night of Jesus' arrest played in the strengthening and settling of Mark's character!

II

"They all forsook Him and fled." O shameful desertion! Not one remained true; all ran for their lives, and left their Master to His fate. Peter, who had so loudly protested his loyalty—he is taking good care not to go to prison and death. James, who with his brother had coveted a seat at Jesus' side—he does not now appear eager for that place. Thomas, who had said, "Let us also go, that we may die with Him"— surely he is facing in the wrong direction. Even John the beloved—Jesus' breast has little charm for him now. They thought only of themselves, not of their Lord, who thought only of them. When He foretold their flight, they all denied indignantly that they could be guilty of such baseness. How much better He knew them than they knew themselves! O my Lord, how often have I joined these fleeing disciples! At my Confirmation I vowed lifelong allegiance to Thee. At the Communion altar, at the beginning of a new year, on birthdays and other anniversaries, on my sickbed, again and again I have repeated my vow. I have said,

"Master, I will follow Thee whithersoever Thou goest"; I have cried, "Lord, to whom shall we go? Thou only hast words of eternal life"; I have sung—

> Jesus, I my cross have taken,
> All to leave and follow Thee.

Yet, O my Lord, how often, despite all, I have left Thee and fled! I have turned away from Thee and given all that I had for my life. I have feared and loved and trusted in men and things rather than in Thee. Forgive my short-lived purposes, my wavering desires, my inconstant mind. Take me back, as Thou didst Thy fleeing disciples. Strengthen, stablish, settle me, as Thou didst Thy servant Mark.

Mark appears to have set down the incident of his flight in a spirit of penitence and faith. He was profoundly ashamed and grieved that he had added to the sins which Jesus had to bear. Yet he rejoiced no less deeply to know that this sin also Jesus had taken away. O my Lord, I would find, like Mark, a place in Thy Gospel. With all my wavering and unworthiness I, too, belong in the history of Thy Passion. I have as good a right there as Mark. Didst not Thou love me and give Thyself for me? Have not I been baptized into Thy death? Thou didst take away the sin of the world, and does not that include mine? Open mine eyes that in the burden of guilt upon Thy shoulder, O Lamb of God, I may discover my sin, my own sin, my own most grievous sin, and cry out in sorrowful and in joyful recognition.

My soul looks back to see
The burden Thou didst bear
When hanging on the cursed Tree,
And knows her guilt was there.

III

For Steadfastness

Lord Jesus Christ, Who in the time of Thy Passion wast forsaken of all Thy friends: Grant that this Thy suffering and desertion may atone for my manifold lapses and goings back. Knit my heart to Thee, and let me nevermore forsake Thee. *Amen.*

In Commemoration of St. Mark

O God, our God, Who having no pleasure in the death of him that dieth, bestowest that grace by which sinners turn and live; Who having once called St. Mark, didst afterwards recall him; and having first blessed him with a believing mother, didst bestow upon him in later life a holy spiritual father, unto the confirmation of his faith and the perfecting of his works; and allottedst unto him for vocation, service with Apostles, and for renown, the name of an Evangelist: Grant us such grace that, having put our hands to the plough, we may not look back; yet, good Lord, if we look back, let mercy excel mercy, and reclaim, renew, restore us. Make our penitence holier than our former sanctity, and our last works more than our first, and our latter end better than our beginning. For His all-prevailing sake, Who alone fell not nor stumbled, Who alone wandered not nor wavered, our Lord Jesus Christ Thy Son. *Amen.*

For Those Who Draw Back From God's Call

O GOD, MERCIFUL AND GRACIOUS, Who callest us unto Thyself in manifold ways, according to the wisdom of Thy loving Providence: Have mercy upon all those who are tempted to draw back from Thy call. Pardon their hesitation, and grant them such love to Thee, that they may not be ensnared by the fascination of the world; faith, that they may not be hindered by its terror; calmness, that they may not be deceived by its excitement; humility, that they may be unshaken by its praise; patience, that they may persevere amid its opposition; hope, that they may press onward to obtain Thy promise; diligence, that they may overcome the infirmity of the flesh; wisdom, that they may clearly perceive what Thou wouldest have them to do; and strength, that they may carry out Thy holy will; through Jesus Christ our Lord. *Amen.*

IV

"MY STRENGTH IS MADE PERFECT IN WEAKNESS"

Once like a broken bow Mark sprang aside:
Yet grace recalled him to a worthier course,
To feeble hands and knees increasing force,
   Till God was magnified.

And now a strong Evangelist, St. Mark
Hath for his sign a Lion in his strength;
And through the stormy water's breadth and length
   He helps to steer God's Ark.

96

FLIGHT

Thus calls he sinners to be penitents,
He kindles penitents to high desire,
He mounts before them to the sphere of saints,
And bids them come up higher.

✠

GOOD JESUS, ABIDE IN ME, AND LET ME ABIDE IN THEE

The Third Thursday

14. THE TRIAL BEFORE THE SANHEDRIN

Be not far from me, for trouble is near: for the assembly of the wicked have inclosed me.

False witnesses are risen up against me: and such as breathe out cruelty.

Mark 14:53, 55-65

(Matt. 26:57, 59-68; Luke 22:54, 63-71)

And they led Jesus away to the high priest: and there come together with Him all the chief priests and the elders and the scribes. Now the chief priests and the whole council sought witness against Jesus to put Him to death; and found it not. For many bare false witness against Him, and their witness agreed not together. And there stood up certain, and bare false witness against Him, saying, We heard Him say, I will destroy this temple that is made with hands, and in three days I will build another made without hands. And not even so did their witness agree together. And the high priest stood up in the midst, and asked Jesus, saying, Answerest Thou nothing? What is it which these witness against Thee? But He held His peace, and answered nothing. Again the high priest asked Him, and saith unto Him, Art thou the Christ, the Son of the Blessed? And Jesus said, I am: and ye shall see the Son of man sitting at the right hand of Power, and coming with the clouds of heaven. And the high priest rent his clothes, and saith, What further need have we of witnesses? Ye have heard the blasphemy: what think ye? And they all condemned Him to be worthy of death. And some began to spit on Him, and to cover His face, and to buffet Him, and to say unto Him, Prophesy: and the officers received Him with blows of their hands.

I

From the manner in which His arrest was brought about it is easy to imagine what sort of justice would await Jesus at His trial. A preliminary hearing in the house of Annas was followed by the formal trial before the Sanhedrin under the presidency of Caiaphas, the high priest. Annas, the aged ex-high priest, still a power through his skill in keeping the sacred office in his family, patron of the temple bazaars with their merchants and money-changers, whom Jesus had driven out; and Caiaphas, his son-in-law, type of the unscrupulous churchman, who had laid down the principle, "It is expedient that one man should die for the people"—what had Jesus to expect from judges such as these?

In keeping with the character of the judges was that of the witnesses, who had all the unscrupulousness of the former with none of their shrewdness. One after another came forward, but it was impossible to base a definite charge on their statements. At last several persons were found who testified to an alleged blasphemous utterance of Jesus concerning the temple; but nothing came of even this promising bit of evidence. Annoyed at the failure of his witnesses and stung by Jesus' silence, the high priest rose and questioned the Prisoner with the object of inducing Him to incriminate Himself. His shameless browbeating

99

was met by Jesus with the silence that it deserved. Caiaphas then suddenly and adroitly shifted his ground. It was necessary to devise and prepare a charge sufficiently broad and grave to assure the unanimous verdict of the Council against Jesus as well as to command the enthusiastic support of the populace. This charge Caiaphas at last found in the messianic claim of Jesus. Reducing the whole indictment against Him to this one count, and putting Him under oath in order to compel a reply, he asked Him if He was the Messiah, "the Son of the Blessed." He paraphrased the second Name, lest perchance he might take it in vain! Jesus replied, "I am"; but carefully qualified His reply, as He did afterwards in answering Pilate's question, "Art Thou a king?" Quoting from Old Testament texts, He made it plain that not in the popular Jewish sense was He the Messiah, but in the sense of the "Son of Man" seen and sung by prophet and psalmist. In pretended horror the high priest rent his garment and hastened the taking of the vote. One after another of the councilors declared Jesus guilty of death. Then the fury of years burst forth. Some of these reverend priests and elders spit on Him, and blindfolding Him struck Him in the face and cried, "Tell us, who was it smote Thee that time—and that—and that!" Then they handed Him over to the attendants, who copied in their ruder fashion the example of their masters.

II

Once more, as at the beginning, O Jesus, Son of the Blessed, Thou art in the midst of the doctors; yet no one is astonished now at Thy understanding and Thy answers. They have put Thee on trial for Thy life; they are determined to find Thee guilty. They bring together false witnesses and lie in wait to entangle Thee in Thy talk. No matter what Thou sayest, they will twist it against Thee. Lo, the high priest has risen and is questioning Thee. O infinite Wisdom, make no reply! Again He questions Thee, He puts Thee under oath, He asks if Thou art the Christ. Now Thou must needs speak. Ah! the good confession, for which everyone that is godly shall praise Thy Name for ever. But it avails Thee not. They cry, "Blasphemy!" and their cries ring through the hall. They are horror-stricken, and yet they are glad. One by one, they condemn Thee to death. O Glory of Thy people Israel! this is the outcome of Thy holy life, Thy gracious words, Thy going about and doing good. Thus do the leaders of Thy people reward Thee. Thou didst come unto Thine own, and Thine own received Thee not.

What a gesture of insincerity was the rending of the high priest's robe! By it Caiaphas stands revealed as an arch-hypocrite. "God shall smite thee, thou whited wall: and sittest thou to judge me according to the law, and commandest me to be smitten contrary to the law?" Thus St. Paul rebuked the high priest Ananias, not knowing that he was high priest. But humbly O my Lord, and in silence Thou dost suffer the falsity of this Thy far more wicked judge. O good Jesus, pure Jesus! keep me from all hypocrisy—lying thoughts, cant words, and insincere acts. Make me to eschew falsity as death eternal. Let me not come under Thy curse, "Woe unto you, hypocrites!" but rather inherit Thy blessing, "Blessed are the pure in heart; for they shall see God."

Verily, O God, Thou makest even the lips of sinful men to praise Thee. Despite himself, this crafty priest uttered a divine truth when he said, "It is expedient that one man should die for the people." Was it not the same truth that Jesus uttered in love and willing obedience—"It is expedient for you that I go away," and "I give my life a ransom for all"? Thus Thou turnest the curse upon men's lips into a blessing, even as Thou didst with Balaam of old. In Thy over-ruling providence Caiaphas, "the high priest that same year," not only proclaimed Thy truth, but himself brought the true Lamb to the offering. Now let him rend his robe; his office and work are ended. So let all Thine enemies perish, O Lord: but let them that love Thee be as the sun when he goeth forth in his might. Let all things work together for good to them that love Thee.

III

For the Merit of Christ's Condemnation

O LORD JESUS CHRIST, Who for my sins wast falsely accused, deliver me, I pray Thee, from the accusation of the law and my own conscience. Thou Who wast silent when false witnesses rose up against Thee, grant that I be not put to confusion at the last judgment. Thou who wast mocked with blows and spitting, save me from everlasting shame and torment. By

Thy most unjust condemnation to death, grant me entrance to life eternal. *Amen.*

"Thou Shalt Not Bear False Witness Against Thy Neighbor"

GRANT US, O LORD OUR GOD, so to fear and love Thee that we may not falsely belie, betray, backbite, or slander our neighbor, but rather excuse him, speak well of him, and put the best construction upon all his actions; through Jesus Christ, our Lord. *Amen.*

For the Falsely Accused

O LORD JESUS CHRIST, Who didst bear the reproach of sin, though Thou hadst done nothing amiss: Have mercy upon all who are falsely accused, and grant them such meekness to bear their trouble, that they may obtain pardon for all their sins, through Thy merits, in the day when Thou shalt judge the secrets of all men. *Amen.*

IV

FROM ANNAS TO CAIAPHAS

Then from one ruler to another, bound,
They lead Me, urging that it was not sound
What I taught: comments would the text confound:
      Was ever grief like Mine?

The Priest and rulers all false witness seek
'Gainst Him Who seeks not life, but is the meek
And ready Paschal Lamb of this great week:
      Was ever grief like Mine?

Then they accuse Me of great blasphemy,
That I did thrust into the Deity,
Who never thought that any robbery:
    Was ever grief like Mine?

Some said that I the Temple to the floor
In three days raz'd and raised as before:
Why, He that built the world can do much more:
    Was ever grief like Mine?

Then they condemn Me all, with that same breath
Which I do give them daily, unto death:
Thus Adam My first breathing rendereth:
    Was ever grief like Mine?

✠

GOOD JESUS, MAKE ME SINCERE

The Third Friday

15. PETER'S DENIAL AND REPENTANCE

If we deny Him; He will also deny us.
If we believe not, yet He abideth faithful: He cannot deny Himself.

Mark 14:54, 66-72

(Matt. 26: 58, 69-75; Luke 22:54-62; John 18:15-18, 25-27)

Peter had followed Him afar off, even within, into the court of the high priest; and he was sitting with the officers, and warming himself in the light of the fire. And as Peter was beneath in the court, there cometh one of the maids of the high priest; and seeing Peter warming himself, she looked upon him, and saith, Thou also wast with the Nazarene, even Jesus. But he denied, saying, I neither know, nor understand what thou sayest; and he went out into the porch; and the cock crew. And the maid saw him and began again to say to them that stood by, This is one of them. But he again denied it. And after a little while again they that stood by said to Peter, Of a truth thou art one of them; for Thou art a Galilæan. But he began to curse, and to swear, I know not this man of whom ye speak. And straightway the second time the cock crew. And Peter called to mind the word, how that Jesus said unto him, Before the cock crow twice, thou shalt deny me thrice. And when he thought thereon, he wept.

I

Mark's account of the denial and repentance of Peter is so rich in personal and realistic detail that it can have come only from Peter himself. Graphically and with many vivid little touches the scene is set before us; thus it was indelibly engraven on Peter's mind. He sat inside the courtyard of Caiaphas, among the attendants, warming himself at the bright fire. Along came a maidservant of the high priest, and observing Peter's lighted face, looked intently upon him and announced that she suspected him to be a follower of Jesus. Peter told her that he did not know what she meant, and wandered out into the passage-way, where the first cockcrow fell unheeded on his ears. The maidservant insisted to the bystanders that he was "one of those people," and again Peter denied it, this time at greater length. After a while the bystanders, convinced that the maid was right, said to him, "To be sure, you belong to them. Why, you are a Galilean!" Then Peter began to curse and to swear—a relapse into an old fisherman's habit—denying that he ever knew "this man," and the second cockcrow sounded.

The three denials present a well-graded climax. At first Peter says evasively, "I have no idea what you are talking about"; then he denies, using many words, that he "belongs to them"; last he says with oaths and curses, "I do not know the man you mean." The double cockcrowing serves but to intensify his guilt. In sharp contrast to the circumstantial account of the sin is the simple notice of the repentance—Peter called to mind the words of Jesus and burst into tears.

Here is the shameful fall of a highly-strung, impulsive character, in surroundings into which he ought never to have ventured, relying proudly on his own strength. Yet it is not difficult to see underneath all the bravado a deep and genuine love for his Lord. That is what distinguished Peter from Judas, though Peter would have been the last to say so. He had learned by bitter experience never again to boast of loving his Master "more than these." The very restraint of his narrative, as contrasted with the other accounts, is a mark of the genuineness of his repentance. John records sorrowfully how he was partially to blame for bringing Peter into temptation. The gentle Luke adds the beautiful picture of Jesus turning and looking on Peter. Both Matthew and Luke tell how Peter went out and wept bitterly. But in Peter's own account, as given by Mark, these extenuating details are omitted; it is his way of saying, "Of whom I am chief." Whenever he told the story of his fall, tears choked his voice, and through his words rang the cry of the psalmist, "Against Thee, Thee only, have I sinned, and done this evil in Thy sight."

II

Good Jesus, when I consider Thy Apostle's fall and bitter weeping, there comes to me a voice saying, "Thou art Peter." "Thou art Peter: thou, too, hast denied thy Lord." Yea, Lord; if Peter denied Thee thrice, I have denied Thee seventy times seven times. I have denied Thee by my words and deeds, I have denied Thee by my silence. I have thought myself secure in my own wisdom and strength, I have refused to listen to Thy words. I have despised the brethren. I have tempted God and run recklessly into danger; I have sat at the world's fire of coals, forgetting that the friendship of the world is enmity with God. I have been deaf to warning voices, and have rushed head-long, like one bereft of reason, from denial to denial. Thou dost bid me deny myself, and take up my cross, and follow Thee; I have denied Thee, flung down my cross, and sworn I was no follower of Thine. I am Peter: I have denied Thee, O my Lord.

"Thou art Peter: on thee, too, does thy Lord look." Ah, the wealth of meaning in that look on Peter! There was in it anger, as when Thou didst look round about on the Pharisees that sabbath day in Capernaum; sorrow, as when Thou didst behold the city and weep over it; affection, as when beholding the young ruler Thou didst love him. No wonder that look broke Peter's heart. Thus dost Thou look also on me—in anger at my sin, in sorrow for my weakness, in love that will not let me go. Thy face looks out on me from the pages of Thy Holy Word: in the Law, to point me to my sin; in the Gospel, to beckon me to Thy side. But nowhere does it shine upon me so clearly as in the Holy Passion—in the garden, in the hall of Caiaphas, in Pilate's palace, and on the Cross; there is the very glory of God in the face of Jesus Christ. I am Peter: Lord Jesus, look also on me!

"Thou art Peter: do thou, too, go out and weep bitterly." Peter's weeping was the beginning of his restoration. The evil night was past, the cockcrow ushered in the new day—the day of Peter's penitence, the day of Jesus' death. Peter went out and wept bitterly; Thou, good Jesus, didst go out and shed Thy blood.

Where these two streams, the tears of the sinner and the blood of the Saviour, meet and mingle, there blossom forgiveness, peace and joy. Let me, too, go out, away from the scene of my fall, into solitude and stillness, and there weep over my sin and call to mind Thy word, Thy look, Thy Cross. Let me go out, not like Judas, in remorse and despair; not in the sorrow of this world that worketh death, but in godly sorrow that worketh repentance to salvation. I am Peter: I have denied Thee, O Lord, my Lord; look on me with the eyes of Thy mercy; send me out to weep tears of repentance, which Thou wilt turn to joy.

III

For the Merciful Look of Jesus

O LORD JESUS CHRIST, Look on me a poor sinner with the eyes of Thy mercy, with which Thou didst look upon Peter in the hall, Mary Magdalen at the feast, and the thief on the cross. Grant, O Almighty Lord, that like Peter I may weep bitterly, like Mary love Thee much, and like the thief be with Thee in Paradise. *Amen.*

For the Tempted

GOOD JESU, Who didst vouchsafe to be tempted as we, to overcome Satan for us and in us: Teach the tempted swiftly to hold to Thee; hold them, lest they fall; raise them, if they give way; cheer them, if they despond; make them to hold tighter to Thee; and never let us for an instant let Thee go, until Thou bless us. *Amen.*

A SHORT LITANY OF REPENTANCE

Lord, have mercy.
Christ, have mercy.
Lord, have mercy.

O God, Who wouldest not the death of a sinner, but his repentance.

Who calledst Adam after his fall to acknowledge his guilt,

Who forgavest the sins of Thy disobedient people at the prayer of Moses,

Who sparedst the Ninevites when they repented,

Who broughtest David to confess his sin, and didst put away his sin upon his confession,

Who sparedst Ahab when he humbled himself,

Who camest into the world to save sinners,

Who heardest the Canaanite when she persevered in prayer,

Who forgavest the many sins of the woman who was a great sinner, because she loved much,

Who broughtest salvation to the house of Zacchaeus, when he restored fourfold,

Who looking upon Peter didst call him to confess his fault and weep bitterly,

Who didst promise Paradise to the penitent thief on the cross,

Who didst bear our sins in Thine own Body on the Tree,

Who after repentance rememberest all our sins no more,
    Have mercy upon me, and spare me, O Lord.

O Lamb of God, That takest away the sin of the world,
    Have mercy upon me, and grant me Thy peace.

OUR FATHER.

IV

GOOD FRIDAY MORN

Peter and James and John,
The sad tale runneth on—
All slept and Thee forgot;
One said He knew Thee not.

110

Peter and James and John,
The sad tale runneth on—
I am that one, the three;
Thus have I done to Thee.

Under a garden wall
I lay at evenfall;
I waked. Thou calledst me;
I had not watched with Thee.

Peter and James and John,
The sad tale runneth on—
By the priest's fagot hot,
I said I knew Thee not.

The little maid spoke out:
"With Him thou wentest about."
"This Man I never met"—
I hear the cock crow yet.

✠

O LOVING JESUS, KNIT ME TO THEE BY THY LOVE

111

The Third Saturday

Judge me, O God: and plead my cause against an ungodly nation.

O deliver me from the deceitful and unjust man: for Thou art the God of my strength.

John 18:28-38

(Matt. 27:1-2, 11-14; Mark 15:1-5; Luke 23:1-4)

They led Jesus therefore from Caiaphas into the Praetorium: and it was early; and they themselves entered not into the Praetorium, that they might not be defiled, but might eat the passover. Pilate therefore went out unto them and saith, What accusation bring ye against this man? They answered and said unto him, If this man were not an evil-doer, we should not have delivered Him up unto thee. Pilate therefore said unto them, Take Him yourselves, and judge him according to your law. The Jews said unto him, It is not lawful for us to put any man to death: that the word of Jesus might be fulfilled, which He spake, signifying by what manner of death He should die.

Pilate therefore entered again into the Praetorium, and called Jesus, and said unto Him, Art Thou the King of the Jews? Jesus answered, Sayest thou this of thyself or did others tell it thee concerning me? Pilate answered, Am I a Jew? Thine own nation and the chief priests delivered Thee unto me: what hast thou done? Jesus answered, My kingdom is not of this world: if my kingdom were of this world, then would my servants fight, that I should not be delivered to the Jews: but now is my kingdom not from hence.

Pilate therefore said unto Him, Art Thou a king then? Jesus answered, Thou sayest that I am a king. To this end have I been born, and to this end am I come into the world, that I should bear witness unto the truth. Every one that is of the truth heareth my voice. Pilate saith unto Him, What is truth? And when he had said this, he went out again unto the Jews, and saith unto them, I find no crime in Him.

I

The trial before Pilate falls into two acts with an interlude. The first act comprises the examination of the charge that Jesus was a royal pretender and closes with the contemptuous dismissal of this charge. The second act consists of Pilate's unsuccessful attempts to rid himself of the responsibility forced upon him by the Jewish authorities—by sending his Prisoner to Herod, by offering the Jews their choice between Jesus and Barabbas, and by a final appeal to the pity of the Crowd—and closes with his reluctant sentence of execution. The warning message of Pilate's wife forms an interlude in the second act. It is the first act that is before us.

In accordance with the Roman policy of provincial government, the Jews were granted a large measure of self-rule, with certain reservations which included the execution of capital sentences. Hence the Sanhedrins were obliged to hand over Jesus to the governor, in order to have their verdict ratified and executed. Scrupulous as always, they refused to enter the heathen praetorium, lest they should become defiled; and this part of the trial took place in the open air. They hoped for a general endorsement of their action without a reopening of the case. But the governor, punctilious as they, insisted that they present the actual charges for his review. They might indeed keep their passover untouched by heathen defilement, but they were not to escape being reminded that they would keep it as Roman subjects.

John passes by the formal presentation of charges; they were well known from the other gospels. Luke gives the most complete enumeration; Jesus is a perverter of the people, He forbids paying tribute to the emperor, and He claims to be Christ a king. The last charge formed the subject of an interview, inside the praetorium, between Pilate and Jesus.

The governor could not bring himself to take the accusation seriously. Scrutinizing his Prisoner from head to foot, he exclaimed, "So you are the King of the Jews!" His words expressed wonder and contempt and pity. Before replying Jesus wished to know in what sense Pilate was using the term "king." He was not merely another of the many rulers of earth, His kingdom did not belong to this world; otherwise His capture would not have been so easy and unbloody a task. "Then you are a king after all?" asked Pilate, and the quiet answer was, "Certainly I am, a king who rules by the truth, and all who belong to the truth are my subjects." "Truth!" said Pilate. "What is that?" And turning his back on Him who is the Truth, and shaking his head over this harmless visionary, he went out and told the Jewish leaders, "For my part, I can find nothing whatever wrong in Him."

II

O Jesus, witnessing a good confession before Pontius Pilate! Thou art the King of glory, O Christ; Thou art the everlasting Son of the Father. Thy kingdom cometh not with observation, but is within the heart: it is not meat and drink, but righteousness, and peace, and joy in the Holy Ghost. Its only law is the royal law of love, its only might is the word of truth. By this word, as by seed in the hand of a sower, it was founded, and though many receive it not or fall away or remain unfruitful, yet like leaven it will permeate the hearts and lives of men, and like the mustard seed overshadow all lands. Men will come upon it unawares, as treasure hidden in a field, or after painful searching, as a pearl of great price, and will give all that they have to possess it. And though it appear now in humble guise and intermingled with much impurity, there will come at last a day of severing, when the righteous shall shine forth as the sun and the wicked be cast into the furnace of fire. Thy kingdom comes wherever the Father's name is hallowed, as it was hallowed by Thee; wherever the Father's will is done, as it was done by Thee. Thy kingdom will come until the kingdoms of this world are become the kingdoms of our Lord and of His Christ. For whoever belongs to the truth shall hear Thy voice, because the Father who sent Thee will draw him. O King, live for ever, and reign in my heart.

O King of truth, Thou art Thyself the Truth, Thy office and person, Thy teaching and life, are one. Thou art full of grace and truth; Thou art the Sinless One, the Spotless Lamb. As the shadows of the Passion deepened about Thee, Thy purity shines with increasing light. "What hast Thou done?" asks Pilate, and himself gives the answer, "I find no fault in Him at all." Herod proclaims Thy innocence by arraying Thee in a shining robe. Judas returns the thirty pieces and confesses that he has betrayed innocent blood. Pilate's wife calls Thee a just person. The penitent thief declares that Thou hast done nothing amiss. The Roman centurion acknowledges Thee to be a righteous man. Thou wast in all points tempted like as we are, yet without sin. Thou knewest no sin. Verily, we are not redeemed with corruptible things, as silver and gold, but with the precious blood of Christ, as of a Lamb without blemish and without spot. May Thy precious blood cleanse us from all our sin. May we whose hope is in Thee, purify ourselves, even as Thou art pure. O Truth, be Thou our Way, be Thou our Life!

III

For a Place in Christ's Kingdom

O LORD JESUS CHRIST, Who for our sins wast tried as an evildoer, let Thy innocent suffering avail for us poor evildoers. Grant us, O King of Grace and Truth, to live under Thee in Thy kingdom of grace, bring us to a fuller knowledge of Thy truth, and receive us at last into Thy kingdom of eternal glory. *Amen.*

"Thy Kingdom Come"

O GOD, WHOSE KINGDOM COMES indeed without our prayer, we pray Thee that it may come also unto us. To this end do Thou, our heavenly Father, give us Thy Holy Spirit, so that by His grace we may believe Thy sacred Word, and live a godly life here on earth and in heaven for ever. Amen.

For Judges and Magistrates

GIVE WISDOM, O Lord, we pray Thee, to all those who are concerned in the habitual correction of the unruly, especially to all our judges and magistrates. Enable them to be diligent in investigation and impartial in judgment, that their word may tend to the diminution of vice and the removal of the principal occasions of evil; and grant that their responsibility for others may lead them to anxious preparation for that sentence which they shall themselves receive from Thee, the Judge of all, and to a faithful acceptance of the means of Thy grace; through Jesus Christ. *Amen.*

IV

"HERZLIEBSTER JESU"

Ah, holy Jesus, how hast Thou offended,
That man to judge Thee hath in hate pretended?
By foes derided, by Thine own rejected,
        O most afflicted.

Who was the guilty? Who brought this upon Thee?
Alas, my treason, Jesus, hath undone Thee.

117

'Twas I, Lord Jesus, I it was denied Thee:
    I crucified Thee.

Lo, the Good Shepherd for the sheep is offered;
The slave hath sinned, and the Son hath suffered;
For man's atonement, while he nothing heedeth.
    God intercedeth.

For me, kind Jesus, was Thine Incarnation,
Thy mortal sorrow, and Thy life's oblation,
Thy death of anguish and Thy bitter Passion,
    For my salvation.

Therefore, kind Jesus, since I cannot pay Thee,
I do adore Thee, and will ever pray Thee,
Think on Thy pity and Thy love unswerving,
    Not my deserving.

✝

JESUS, BE THOU THE MASTER OF MY THINKING
AND THE LORD OF MY LIFE

The Third Monday

17. THE TRAITOR'S END

*Whither shall I go from Thy spirit: or whither shall
I flee from Thy presence?*

*If I say, Surely the darkness shall cover me: even
the night shall be light about me.*

Yea, the darkness hideth not from Thee.

Matthew 27:3-10

(Acts 1:16-25)

Then Judas, who betrayed Him, when he saw that He
was condemned, repented himself, and brought back
the thirty pieces of silver to the chief priests and elders
saying, I have sinned in that I betrayed innocent
blood. But they said, What is that to us? See thou to
it. And he cast down the pieces of silver into the sanctuary and departed; and he went away and hanged
himself. And the chief priests took the pieces of silver,
and said, It is not lawful to put them into the treasury,
since it is the price of blood. And they took counsel,
and bought with them the Potter's Field, to bury
strangers in. Wherefore that field was called the field
of blood, unto this day. Then was fulfilled that which
was spoken through Jeremiah the prophet, saying,
And they took the thirty pieces of silver, the price
of him that was priced, whom certain of the children of Israel did price; and they gave them for the
Potter's Field, as the Lord appointed me.

I

Where the traitor spent the interval between the arrest
of Jesus and His condemnation is not known; but on

the morning of Good Friday he suddenly reappeared. The knowledge that Jesus had been sentenced to death and was being handed over to the governor had produced in him a deep revulsion of feeling; now only did he begin to realize the enormity of his crime. Matthew says that he repented, but the word he uses is not the great New Testament term "repent"; it denotes merely "to change one's mind" or "to be sorry," which is something very different from the profound change of heart and purpose involved in genuine repentance.

In this mood Judas came running up, while the priests and elders were on the way with their Prisoner to the governor's palace, or while they were waiting outside during Pilate's first examination of Jesus. He offered to return the silver pieces; he acknowledged that he had done wrong, and bore witness to the innocence of his Lord. But his words fell on deaf ears. Those priests and elders had done with him; like an outworn garment they flung him aside. "What does that matter to us? It is your affair"—thus they paraphrased the question of Cain. Then rage and despair took possession of Judas. Rushing off to the temple, up to the door of the Holy Place, he hurled the accursed money far within. They shall have it back, whether they will or no! From there he wandered away, like one driven by furies, and finally put an end to his intolerable life.

Various conflicting tales were told, among the shuddering disciples, about the traitor's end, two of which found their way into the New Testament. They agreed in connecting the death of Judas with the "Field of Blood." The coins were found on the temple floor, and even if Judas had not been seen hurling them down, their number would betray whose they were. The matter came up at a session of the Sanhedrin, and it was decided with characteristic hypocrisy that it would be wrong to put the "price of blood" into the Lord's treasury. Nevertheless, the money found in the sanctuary must be regarded as given for a sacred purpose. Finally some one discovered a sufficiently pious use for it, namely, the purchase of a plot of ground for a "Potter's Field," to be used as a burial place for visitors from abroad, especially festival pilgrims, overtaken by death in the holy city. Thus the "Potter's Field" came to be known as the "Field of Blood," which name it bore when our first gospel was composed.

II

Lord Jesus, trembling and amazed I stand before this mystery of iniquity; I hide my face and fear to look upon the "son of perdition." Yet his fate may well be to me a wholesome warning. Poor, pitiful lost soul! In his anguish of heart and despair of God's mercy he turned for help to his own wisdom and strength, to the counsel of men, everywhere but to the One who alone is able to save to the uttermost.

When my sins overwhelm me, let me not seek for comfort in my own heart. That way lies not relief, but only despair. What else could Judas find, when he looked into his heart, but the memory of a misspent life, the reproaches of an accusing conscience, the help-

lessness of a broken will? Though he "repented" and
came to himself, it was the same old Judas he came to.
When the Prodigal Son in Thy parable came to himself, he said, "I will arise, and go to my Father." Show
me, O Lover of men, that in me dwelleth no good
thing. Teach me that, as long as I live, all dependence
on self must end in the lament, "O wretched man
that I am! who shall deliver me from the body of this
death?"

Neither let me turn to the wisdom and counsel of
men. Judas indeed confessed his fault and acknowledged his Lord's innocence, but he made an ill choice
of confessors. Depraved priests and callous elders, what
help could he expect from them? With a shrug of their
shoulders they washed their hands of him and sent
him on his headlong way. Even good friends can
avail but little when the soul cries out of the depths;
human counsel and affection are but broken reeds to
lean upon. Surely men of low degree are but vanity,
and men of high degree are a lie: to be laid in the balance, they are altogether lighter than vanity. O my
Lord, I would trust in Thee at all times. Thou art my
refuge and strength. Let me turn to Thee alone, when
trouble and heaviness take hold upon me and Satan
would drive me to despair. If only Judas had fled to
Thee, remembering Thy word, "Him that cometh to
me I will in no wise cast out"! Thou wouldst have received him with open arms, as Thou didst the penitent
thief. If my heart condemn me, Thou art greater than
my heart, and knowest all things. If friends forsake me
and foes deride, Thou wilt never leave me, so that I

need not fear what man shall do unto me. Let me look away from self, from my sins and from my good works as well; away from men and the ways of men. Let me set Thy Cross before me, and say, "Thou, Lord Jesus, art my righteousness, and I am Thy sin; Thou hast taken upon Thee what was mine, and given me what is Thine. I will know nothing save Thee, and Thee crucified." If Thou, sweet Jesus, wilt grant me this, then neither death nor life, nor angels, nor principalities, nor powers, nor things present, nor things to come, nor height, nor depth, nor any other creature, shall be able to separate me from the love of God, which is in Thee, Christ Jesus, in Thee, our Lord.

III

"Lead Us Not Into Temptation"

O GOD, WHO TEMPTEST NO ONE TO SIN, we pray Thee so to guard and preserve us that the devil, the world, and our own flesh may not deceive us, nor lead us into error, unbelief, despair, and other great and shameful sins; and that, though we be thus tempted, we may finally prevail and gain the victory; through Jesus Christ Thy Son our Lord. *Amen.*

Against Despair of God's Mercy

WE CONFESS UNTO THEE, Almighty God, that we have deserved Thy righteous wrath and manifold punishments; yet we entreat Thee, O most merciful Father, remember not the sins of our youth, nor our many transgressions, but out of Thine unspeakable goodness, grace, and mercy, defend us from all harm and danger of body and soul. Preserve us from false and pernicious doctrine, from anguish of heart and despair of Thy mercy, and from an evil death. And in every time of trouble show Thyself a very present Help, the Saviour of all men, and especially of them that believe; for the sake of the bitter sufferings and death of Jesus Christ, Thine only Son our Lord. *Amen.*

FOR A HOLY LIFE AND A CHRISTIAN CLOSE

The Angel of peace, a faithful guide, guardian of souls and bodies, to encamp around us, and ever to prompt what is salutary,
> Vouchsafe, O Lord.

Pardon and remission of all sins and of all offences,
> Vouchsafe, O Lord.

Repentance and strictness for the residue of our life, and health and peace to the end,
> Vouchsafe, O Lord.

Whatever is true, whatever is honest, whatever just, whatever pure, whatever lovely, whatever of good report, if there be any virtue, if any praise, such thoughts, such deeds,
> Vouchsafe, O Lord

A Christian close without sin, without shame, and should it please Thee, without pain, and a good answer at the dreadful judgment seat of Jesus Christ our Lord,
> Vouchsafe, O Lord.

IV

THE DARK ANGEL

Dark Angel, with thine aching lust
  To rid the world of penitence:
Malicious Angel, who still dost
  My soul such subtile violence!

Because of thee, no thought, no thing,
  Abides for me undesecrate:
Dark Angel, ever on the wing,
  Who never reachest me too late!

Thou art the whisper in the gloom,
  The hinting tone, the haunting laugh:
Thou art the adorner of my tomb,
  The minstrel of mine epitaph.

I fight thee, in the Holy Name!
  Yet, what thou dost is what God saith:
Tempter should I escape thy flame,
  Thou wilt have helped my soul from Death:

The second Death, that never dies,
  That cannot die, when time is dead;
Live Death, wherein the lost soul cries,
  Eternally uncomforted.

Do what thou wilt, thou shalt not so,
  Dark Angel, triumph over me:
Lonely, unto the Lone I go;
  Divine, to the Divinity.

☩

O LORD, LEAVE ME NOT TO MYSELF

The Third Tuesday

---

*Then shall they call upon me, but I will not answer:
they shall seek me early, but they shall not find me.
    For that they hated knowledge: and did not choose
the fear of the Lord.*

Luke 23:5-12

But they were the more urgent, saying, He stirreth
up the people, teaching throughout all Judæa, and beginning from Galilee even unto this place. But when
Pilate heard it, he asked whether the man were a
Galilæan. And when he knew that He was of Herod's
jurisdiction, he sent Him unto Herod, who himself
also was at Jerusalem in these days. Now when Herod
saw Jesus, he was exceeding glad: for he was of a long
time desirous to see Him, because he had heard concerning Him; and he hoped to see some miracle done
by Him. And he questioned Him in many words; but
He answered him nothing. And the chief priests and
the scribes stood, vehemently accusing Him. And
Herod with his soldiers set Him at nought, and
mocked Him, and arraying Him in gorgeous apparel
sent Him back to Pilate. And Herod and Pilate became friends with each other that very day: for before they were at enmity between themselves.

I

Here is the most revolting incident in the trial narrative. Herod, infamous son of an infamous father, who
lived in adultery with his brother's wife, whom Jesus

called "that fox," before whom Salome danced, and who gave the drunken order to strike off John Baptist's head—Herod and Jesus face to face! The tetrarch was overjoyed at the meeting. For a long time he had wished to see this man. He had been haunted by the spectre of the murdered Baptist, and at times half believed Jesus was that prophet returned to life. He had heard many things about Him, and had been hoping to see some miracle performed by Him, something startling and unheard of, to stir his jaded mind.

Now, by a happy chance, Jesus stood before him, and eagerly the king plied Him with questions. But all the answer he got from Him was silence. Why should he speak? What should He say? At the close of verse 9—"He answered him nothing"—an ancient manuscript adds, "as if He had not been there," and another old text reads, "as if He did not hear." Deeper and deeper grew the silence of Jesus, and into it the king's chatter dropped, as into a deep well, and was lost, and soon there was not a sound in the room. Two speechless kings faced each other. Slowly Herod began to understand the meaning of Jesus' silence; it clamored in his ears more loudly than the Baptist's rebuke. The rôles were reversed; it was no longer Jesus before Herod; it was Herod before Jesus. But not for long. Gathering the shreds of his royalty about him, Herod stamped his foot in fury. There shall be no more silence! He summoned his men of war, and together they filled the hall with their shouts and laughter, as they mocked and derided the silent Christ.

Having vented his petty vengeance on our Lord, Herod set himself to return the courtesy of Pilate. The governor had sent Jesus to Herod, thus gracefully recognizing his jurisdiction. Herod in turn magnanimously refused to interfere in the case and remitted Him to Pilate. In a spirit of friendly raillery he sent Jesus back dressed in a splendid robe. "Here you have your king again. I leave the case in your capable hands." That day governor and tetrarch, between whom a coldness had sprung up, became again good friends.

II

Jesus, silent in the palace of Herod! in how strange and terrifying a guise dost Thou appear! The Word has no word, He who came to reveal God keeps silence, He who spake as never man spake holds His peace. In the coasts of Tyre and Sidon Thou wast silent to the woman of Canaan; when she cried to Thee for mercy on her demon-ridden daughter, Thou answeredst her not a word. But that was the silence of love. Its purpose was to cause her to redouble her entreaty, and to attend the more closely to Thy words when Thou shouldest speak. Reading Thy silence aright, she fell down before Thee and prayed the more fervently; she listened hungrily for the sound of Thy voice; she seized upon the humiliating reference in the little word "dogs" and most skilfully turned the argument against Thee even as Thou waited for her to do. Thus didst Thou lead her faith from strength to strength, until it was even marvelous in Thine eyes and Thou couldest grant her whatsoever she would. Good Jesus, if Thou art pleased to be silent to me, let it be with the golden silence of Thy love. May it lead me to cry day and night unto Thee without ceasing, to give the closer heed to all Thy sayings, and to grow in faith, so that I may obtain from Thee what I will. Let me have Thy Word as a true possession, so that I may be able also to hear Thy silence.

But Thy silence, O Lord, at the court of Herod is the silence of judgment. Thou hast nothing to say to this abandoned king. Thou wilt not cast Thy pearls before swine, nor give that which is holy unto dogs of this breed. Of all men most miserable, he is the only person that met Thee face to face, and spoke to Thee, yet never heard Thy voice. There was no greeting, there was no farewell. When he questioned Thee in many words, Thou madest no reply. When the priests accused Thee and the soldiers mocked Thee, Thou didst not open Thy mouth. When they dressed Thee up in a gorgeous robe, Thou sufferedst it in silence. When they led Thee back to Pilate, Thou didst follow without a word. Speechless as Thou hadst come Thou wentest away. It was the silence of judgment, a foretaste and beginning of everlasting condemnation, when the silence of the Judge will thunder, "Depart from me!" Men have sought to portray the horror of eternal torment under various images—an endless burning lake or illimitable fields of ice; but more terrible is the picture of hell as the place of the silence of God, broken only by the sound of weeping and gnashing of teeth. Unto Thee will I cry, O Lord, my Rock; be not silent to me: lest, if Thou be silent to me, I become like them that go down into the pit.

III

"Jesus, Thy Blood and Righteousness"

O LORD JESUS, Who being innocent wast falsely accused and condemned to death, let Thy innocence atone for my guilt. O Thou Who didst patiently endure injustice, let Thy patience overcome my disobedience, and be my pattern as I strive to follow Thee. Let the shining robe in which Thou wast arrayed cover my sins, that I may stand at last before Thy throne clothed with a white robe, and sing Thy praise for ever. *Amen.*

A Pleading for the Sensual and Self-Indulgent

BE MERCIFUL AND GRACIOUS, O Lord, unto Thy servants, and pardon the infirmities of our earthly nature. Grant that all they who are especially hindered in their spiritual course by the appetites of the flesh (particularly . . .) may be quickened by the power of Thy Holy Spirit and strengthened in all holy endeavors, so that they may bring their bodies into subjection, and living in watchful observance of Thy holy laws, may be delivered by Thy grace from this body of death; through Jesus Christ our Saviour. *Amen.*

A THANKSGIVING FOR ANSWERED PRAYER

I love the Lord
Because He hath heard my voice and my supplication.

Because He hath inclined His ear unto me, therefore will I
   call upon Him as long as I live.
He hath not despised nor abhorred the affliction of the afflicted,
Neither hath He hid His face from him, but when he cried
   unto Him, He heard.
Blessed be the Lord,
Because He hath heard the voice of my supplications.
If I regard iniquity in my heart, the Lord will not hear me.
But verily, God hath heard me, He hath attended to the voice
   of my prayer.
Blessed be God,
Who hath not turned away my prayer, nor His mercy from
   me.
Therefore, my soul, be joyful in the Lord, and rejoice in His
   salvation.

IV

BEFORE HEROD

Dismissed by Pilate, see thy most just Judge
   From this judge most unjust, led to a king
Much more unjust. Lo, how He's forced to trudge
   Through thick and thin; hark how their clamors ring
      About His ears! and see the people flock
      To see whereat to wonder, gaze, and mock!

To Herod come, that long had longed to see Him,
   See now (as if some juggler He had been,
That would show tricks to all men that would fee Him)
   How he provokes Him some trick to begin:
      But, for He silent stands and thwarts his mind,
      He holds Him but a fool, and fool unkind.

How mute was He among so many lies,
   Loud lies, God wot, brayed out by His accusers!
How still, meek Lamb, among so many cries

THE MAN OF SORROWS

Of foul-mouthed hounds, His hunters and abusers!
In few, He showed so many gifts of grace,
That men might clearly see God in His face.

✤

LORD, BE NOT SILENT TO ME

The Fourth Wednesday

19. THE DREAM OF PILATE'S WIFE

I remember Thee upon my bed: I meditate on Thee in the night watches.

Thou art fairer than the children of men: grace is poured out in Thy lips; therefore God hath blessed Thee for ever.

Matthew 27:19

And while Pilate was sitting on the judgment-seat, his wife sent unto him, saying, Have thou nothing to do with that righteous man; for I have suffered many things this day in a dream because of Him.

I

This little interlude seems at first glance to be out of place in Matthew's narrative, and to belong rather in that of Luke with its feminine element and its preference for the tender aspects of the Gospel, where it would form a companion piece to the weeping daughters of Jerusalem. Upon more careful study, however, it is seen to fit admirably into the first gospel, in which Jesus is presented as Jewish Messiah rejected by His own people and accepted by Gentiles. This motif may be traced through the whole of Matthew's narrative, from the visit of the magi to the confession of the centurion on Calvary. In this chronicle of the shame of Israel, this prophecy of the world-wide scope of the

Gospel, the episode of Pilate's wife finds a proper place.

The whole Jewish nation was bent on destroying its Messiah; not one voice was raised in His defence. The only testimony in His favor came from the house of the heathen governor. Jesus' disciples had forsaken Him, the chief priests and elders had condemned Him as an evildoer, the people demanded His death. This woman alone took His part and called Him a righteous man. In the struggle for Pilate's soul she stood on the side of the heavenly powers. With singular daring and feminine disregard for law she sent to her husband-judge, in the midst of the trial, a message intended to influence him in favor of the Prisoner. She told him of a troubled dream she had had during the past night, in which Jesus appeared to her, and she besought him to wash his hands of the whole iniquitous affair. Dreams reflect our waking thoughts, and the dream of Pilate's wife betrayed her deep interest in "that righteous man." By thus referring to Jesus she recalled to her husband a recent conversation between them in which His person and fate had been discussed. Well would it have been for Pilate had he listened to her warning. She spoke as the ally of his better nature.

II

I observe in the story of Pilate's wife, first of all, the warning of a loving spouse. If Herodias was Herod's evil genius, Pilate's wife was her husband's good angel. How much truer was her insight than his, how much

simpler and more direct her mind! She put his welfare
above her own, and braved a sharp rebuke in order to
save him from a dreadful mistake. If he had listened
to her, his name would not stand, immortalized in
shame, in the Church's oldest creed. Her warning was
the act of a true helpmate. Alas, that it failed! I see
here the duty of loved ones to each other—of husband
and wife, parents and children, lovers and friends. St.
Paul says, "What knowest thou, O wife, whether thou
shalt save thy husband? or how knowest thou, O
man, whether thou shalt save thy wife?" Love and
friendship reach their full stature only when they are
hallowed by a right relation to Christ. O my Lord, am
I acting as good angel to those bound to me by ties of
affection? Have I raised a warning voice when loved
ones were about to sin against their Lord?

Again, I notice the tribute of a daughter of Rome.
When the women of Israel were silent, this heathen
woman bore witness to the innocence of Jesus. The
daughters of Jerusalem wept and lamented as they followed Him on His way to the Cross, but this Roman
lady used her influence to save Him from that way.
Her failure in no wise diminishes the fineness of her
deed. It shines like a gleam of sunshine in a dark day.
When Jesus stood before the elders, His chief apostle
denied Him with oaths and curses; in the trial before
Pilate this stranger pleaded His cause. She had not
known the precious reality of His presence for years
together, as Peter had and the rest; to her He was but
a dream. Yet how she put them all to shame! It is a
prophecy, good Jesus, that Thou shalt never lack for

friends, that Thou shalt sprinkle many nations. Always there will come from distant land testimonials to Thy goodness, wreaths woven by black and brown and yellow fingers for Thy brow. Let me bestir myself, that my witness give no uncertain sound, lest I be put to shame by those that are without.

Lastly, I find here the yearning of a noble heathen. The dream of Pilate's wife is an epitome of the dreams and longings of the heathen world, its age-long hope of a righteous man, a Saviour. From the beginning thinkers and poets and simple saints have dreamed of One fairer than the children of men and have caught glimpses of His far-off face. My Saviour, Thou art the Desire of the nations, the Hope of all the ends of the world. For Thee the isles do wait. Lifted up from the earth, Thou wilt draw all men unto Thee, and wilt put their best dreams to shame. What am I doing to make those dreams come true? Have I devoted as I should my interest, my gifts, my prayers, myself, to this high cause? Can I say with Paul, "Whom ye ignorantly worship, Him declare I unto you"? Make me to see, good Jesus, that the measure of my response to the dream of the heathen world is the measure of the reality with which Thou rulest my own life.

III

LITANY FOR THE CONVERSION OF ALL MEN

O God the Father in Heaven,
O God the Son, Redeemer of the world,
O God the Holy Ghost, the Comforter,

O holy and blessed Trinity, three in one and one in three,
Have mercy upon us.

From having other gods before Thee, the only God,
From blasphemy of Thy holy Name, with our lips or in our
lives,
From neglect of Thy presence in the assembly of Thy people,
by irregular attendance or wandering thoughts,
From want of reverence to parents and others that have au-
thority over us,
From malice and hatred, from party-spirit and vindictiveness,
From all impurity, whether in thought, word, or deed,
From falsehood and injustice in contracts and promises, from
false pretences and theft,
From sneering and disparagement, from exaggeration and
slander,
From idleness, from all discontent with our own position,
and from envy and covetousness.
Good Lord, deliver us.

By the mystery of Thy holy Incarnation,
By Thy Birth and subjection to the law,
By Thine obedience to Thy parents, and by the toil of Thy
poverty,
By Thy Baptism, Fasting, and Temptation,
By Thine endurance of contradiction, and by Thy compassion
for Thine enemies,
By Thy watching in prayer, Thine Agony and bloody Sweat,
By Thy Cross and Passion, by Thy Death and Burial,
By Thy glorious Resurrection and Ascension,
By Thy heavenly Intercession, and the gift of the Holy Ghost,
Help us, good Lord.

We poor sinners do beseech Thee
To hear us, good Lord.
And to provide Thy Church with all that is needful for the
accomplishment of Thy work in the conversion of souls,
To increase the number of those who labor in Thy vineyard,

To stir up the zeal of all Thy people, for the promotion of every good work,

To supply whatever is wanting to Thy Church, and to amend whatever is amiss in her,

To raise up among us a deeper sense of truth and justice in commercial dealings one toward another,

To strengthen in the habits of industry all who are called to manual labor,

To make employers more careful on behalf of those who serve them,

To fill with Thy true knowledge all who have the education of youth,

To cleanse our cities from all impurity, revelry, and unseemliness,

To extend the knowledge of Christ to those who have it not,

To bless all existing missions, and to increase their number,

To have mercy upon all who are in error, and to bring them into the way of Thy truth.

To bless all Christian nations, purifying them from every taint of infidelity or superstition, and perfecting them in the faith,

To make all nations to be at peace with one another,

To fulfill Thy promise that, lifted up from the earth, Thou wilt draw all men unto Thee,

To hasten the day of Thine appearing, and to give us meanwhile earnest love and longing for the same,

We beseech Thee to hear us, good Lord.

O Lamb of God, That takest away the sin of the world,

Have mercy upon us, and grant us Thy peace.

Our Father

For the Heathen

O GOD OF ALL THE NATIONS OF THE EARTH: Remember the multitudes of the heathen who, though created in Thine image, are perishing in their igno-

rance, and according to the propitiation of Thy Son
Jesus Christ, grant that by the prayers and labors of
Thy Holy Church they may be delivered from all superstition and unbelief, and brought to worship Thee;
through Him Whom Thou hast sent to be our Salvation, the Resurrection and the Life of all the faithful,
the same Thy Son Jesus Christ our Lord. *Amen*.

IV

PILATE'S WIFE

Why came in dreams the low-born man
   Between thee and thy rest?
For vain thy whispered message ran,
   Though justice was thy quest.

Did some young ignorant angel dare—
   Not knowing what must be,
Or blind with agony of care—
   To fly for help to thee?

It may be. Rather I believe,
   Thou, nobler than thy spouse,
The rumored grandeur didst receive,
   And sit with pondering brows,

Until thy maidens' gathered tale
   With possible marvel teems:
Thou sleepest, and the Prisoner pale
   Returneth to thy dreams.

Well mightst thou suffer things not few
   For His sake all the night!
In pale eclipses He suffers, who
   Is of the world the light.

139

THE MAN OF SORROWS

Precious it were to know thy dream
  Of such a one as He!
Perhaps of Him we, waking, deem
  As poor a verity.

✤

JESUS, REST OF THE RESTLESS, MAY OUR RESTLESSNESS
FIND REST IN THEE

The Fourth Thursday

20. JESUS BARABBAS OR JESUS CHRIST

---

*And a man of Belial said, We have no part in David:
neither have we inheritance with the son of Jesse.
    Ye denied the Holy One and the Just: and desired
a murderer to be granted unto you.*

Matthew 27:15-18, 20-23

(Mark 15:6-14; Luke 23:13-23; John 18:39-40)

Now at the feast the governor was wont to release
unto the multitude one prisoner, whom they would.
And they had then a notable prisoner, called Barabbas.
When therefore they were gathered together, Pilate
said unto them, Whom will ye that I release unto
you? Barabbas, or Jesus who is called Christ? For
he knew that for envy they had delivered Him up.
Now the chief priests and the elders persuaded the
multitudes that they should ask for Barabbas, and
destroy Jesus. But the governor answered and said
unto them, Which of the two will ye that I release
unto you? And they said, Barabbas. Pilate saith unto
them, What then shall I do unto Jesus who is called
Christ? They all say, Let Him be crucified. And he
said, Why, what evil hath He done? But they cried
out exceedingly, saying, Let Him be crucified.

I

Pilate's attempt to rid himself of his troublesome Prisoner by sending Him to Herod had failed; Jesus was
back again and with the governor lay the decision.

141

His next step was to shift the responsibility upon the people and compel them to make the choice he had not the courage to make. To this end he invoked an old passover custom according to which the Roman governor released every year a Jewish prisoner under sentence of death. The people were permitted to select the prisoner to be released and in order to make sure that they would designate Jesus, Pilate limited their choice to two men. They were to decide between the man in whom neither the governor nor the tetrarch could find any fault, and the notorious Barabbas, a robber, seditionist, and murderer.

There is a striking variant in a number of manuscripts of Matthew's gospel, which has won the approval of several New Testament scholars and editors. According to this reading Barabbas's first name was Jesus. This was by no means an uncommon name among the Jews, and more than one bearer of it meets us in the Old Testament and in the New. The similarity of names may have had something to do with Pilate's selection of Barabbas rather than one of the two other malefactors crucified with our Lord. In this way he was able to sharpen the contrast between the two prisoners, and to set the issue dramatically before the people. "Which Jesus of the two do you wish me to set free—Jesus Barabbas, the insurrectionist and murderer, or Jesus Christ, who has done no wrong?"

No one can tell what the outcome would have been if the priests and elders, blinded with envy and bent on destroying Jesus Christ, had not incited the crowd to ask for Jesus Barabbas. Pilate was completely taken

142

aback by their choice. We can detect his disappointment and his perplexity in the reply, "Then what am I to do with Jesus who is called Christ?" The docile crowd had their answer ready, "Send Him to the cross!" Crying down the governor's half-hearted remonstrance, "Why what wrong has He done?" they went on shouting the more loudly, "Send Him to the cross!" Thus Pilate's plans were foiled once more, and Israel denied the Holy One and the Just and desired a murderer to be granted unto them.

II

Good Jesus, I kneel before Thee numbered with transgressors, and accounted by Thy people as more deserving of death than the vilest criminal. Thou who thoughtest it not robbery to be equal with God art held lower than a robber. O Prince of Peace and Bringer of Life, Thou art rejected for an inciter to riot and a murderer. Oh, the blindness, the sinful folly of men! How terrible the guilt of those wicked leaders, how pitiable the ignorance of that fickle populace! Was there in all that crowd, shouting itself hoarse before the governor's palace, no one with courage enough to stand up for the right? Arm me, O Lord, against the arguments of leaders who are not led by Thee; keep me from being swept along by the unthinking multitude. In every time of choosing let me say with Thy servant of old, "As for me and my house, we will serve the Lord." Nay, is not the choice before me every day? As long as the flesh lusteth against the spirit, and the spirit against the flesh, it is ever "Jesus or Barab-

bas." Let me send Barabbas to the cross by crucifying
the flesh with its affections and lusts, and obtain my
Lord's release by living and walking in the Spirit.

Blessed Saviour, I behold in Barabbas a mirror of
my own guilt and deliverance. He has committed
many crimes, he is justly condemned to die. Even now
the cross is being cut, on which he must hang. With
his fellow criminals he is awaiting in prison the hour
of death. The door flies open, the executioner appears.
Now, Barabbas, thy last hour is come. But see! his fet-
ters are struck off, he is led out dazed into the sun-
light, and scarcely trusting his ears he is told that he is
free. How is this? Why, another has been found, another Jesus, to take thy place and hang upon thy cross.
Thou art guilty, Barabbas, as everyone knows; yet
thou art set free. Jesus Christ—has not the governor
repeatedly declared it?—has done nothing wrong; yet
He must die. Oh, wondrous substitution! Even so all
we like sheep have gone astray; we have turned every
one to his own way; and the Lord hath laid on Him
the iniquity of us all. Our soul is escaped as a bird out
of the snare of the fowlers; the snare is broken, and we
are escaped. Good Jesus, true Jesus, Who wilt save Thy
people from their sins, be my Jesus, and save me, and
make me Thine.

III

For Grace to Make a Right Choice

Oh, THE GRIEF, LORD JESUS, that Thy people
brought upon Thee, when they rejected their Saviour

144

and Christ and chose a murderer, casting away their life and salvation and preferring death and a curse! O Lord, evermore preserve us, by Thy good Spirit, from this sin; grant us to choose Thee, and in Thee life and salvation. Keep us ever mindful that in Thee alone is health and peace, so that cleaving to Thee in unwavering faith we may attain at last to heavenly and eternal joys; for Thy sake and through Thy bitter pains. *Amen.*

Away With Barabbas! Give us Jesus!

Lord Jesus, we adore Thy love, and we entreat Thee to make us partakers of its benefits. Deliver us from half-hearted service, and establish our hearts in Thy grace. Cause us to abhor and flee from inconstancy and lukewarmness; keep us from the sin of Pilate. We are guilty, O Lord, of Thy blood; for our sake it was shed unto the remission of sins. Teach us to hate and forsake the sin that brought Thee to the Cross. Be it our life, O Surety, to love Thee; our glory, O Winner of our freedom, to serve Thee. Protect and guard us that we may not choose Barabbas, nor ever cry in word or deed, "Away with this Man!" Yea, Lord, abide with us; dwell, walk, rule Thou within us. Behold in us of the travail of Thy soul, and be satisfied. *Amen.*

Intercession for the Inconstant

O everlasting god, Who changest not, and Who canst do everything: Have mercy upon all who halt

upon both sides and cannot choose whom they will
serve. Forgive them their inconstancy, reject them not
because they will not accept Thee, choose them though
they have not chosen Thee. Bring them to a penitent
sense of their blindness and sin, and so shine in their
hearts, giving them the light of the knowledge of Thy
glory in the face of Jesus Christ, that they may yield
themselves wholly to Thee, and abiding faithful unto
the end may receive of Thee a crown of life; through
the same Jesus Christ our only Saviour. *Amen.*

IV

A VISION OF LIFE IN DEATH

In evil long I took delight,
   Unawed by shame or fear,
Till a new object struck my sight,
   And stopp'd my wild career:
I saw One hanging on a Tree
   In agonies and blood,
Who fix'd His languid eyes on me,
   As near His Cross I stood.

Sure never, till my latest breath
   Can I forget that look:
It seem'd to charge me with His death,
   Though not a word He spoke:
My conscience felt and own'd the guilt,
   And plunged me in despair;
I saw my sins His Blood had spilt,
   And help'd to nail Him there.

Alas! I know not what I did!
   But now my tears are vain:

146

JESUS BARABBAS OR JESUS CHRIST

Where shall my trembling soul be hid?
   For I the Lord have slain!
A second look He gave, which said,
   "I freely all forgive;
This Blood is for thy ransom paid;
   I die, that thou may'st live."

Thus, while His death my sin displays
   In all its blackest hue,
Such is the mystery of grace,
   It seals my pardon, too.
With pleasing grief, and mournful joy,
   My spirit now is fill'd,
That I should such a life destroy—
   Yet live by Him I kill'd!

☩

LORD, CHOOSE ME, THAT I MAY CHOOSE THEE

The Fourth Friday

21. "HIS BLOOD BE ON US AND ON OUR CHILDREN"

The ox knoweth his owner, and the ass his master's crib: but Israel doth not know, my people doth not consider.

He came unto His own: and His own received Him not.

Matthew 27:24-25

When Pilate saw that he prevailed nothing, but rather that a tumult was arising, he took water, and washed his hands, before the multitude, saying, I am innocent of the blood of this righteous man; see ye to it. And all the people answered and said, His blood be on us, and on our children.

I

When Pilate's second attempt to free Jesus had failed and he perceived that the ugly mood of the crowd threatened to break out at any moment into serious rioting, he literally washed his hands of the case, declaring by word and action, "I am innocent of this good man's death; it is your affair." Here we have the most dramatic confession of our Lord's sinlessness. Pilate was not merely echoing the words of his wife when he called Him "this good man," but bore witness to the profound impression Jesus had made upon his own conscience. And yet it was a confession of impotence, a sorry admission of defeat. Instead of acting upon his conviction and using his hands to set this good man free, he poured water upon them and delivered Him up to the popular will. Blinded with fury and lusting for blood, the crowd declared its readiness to assume full responsibility for Jesus' death.

In the crowd there must have been many who were familiar with the ceremony of hand-washing—one of the rites prescribed in the Jewish law. When, for example, an untraced murder was committed in one of the cities of refuge, the elders of the city solemnly washed their hands as a disclaimer of guilt, and the priests responded with the prayer, "Be merciful, O Lord, unto Thy people Israel, whom Thou hast redeemed, and lay not innocent blood unto Thy people Israel's charge." Now, however, in response to Pilate's washing of his hands came the awful cry, like a chant from some infernal liturgy, "His blood be on us, and on our children." Thus Israel sealed its rejection of the Messiah, for whose sake alone the nation existed. It was the suicide of the chosen people, following upon Pilate's words, "It is your affair," just as the suicide of the chosen disciple followed when the same words were uttered by the chief priests. Terribly was that innocent blood required at their hands, when a generation later the Romans came and took away their place and nation, burnt their temple, and laid the holy city even with the ground.

II

Black as was the guilt of Pilate, O Lord of love, the sin of Thy people was blacker still. Though weak as water, he strove to persuade them of Thy innocence and to obtain Thy release; they, flesh of Thy flesh and bone of Thy bone, not only insisted upon Thy death but in incredible madness called down Thy Blood upon themselves and their children. How dreadfully that cry was answered, that curse fulfilled! The king sent forth His armies, and destroyed those murderers, and burned up their city. But, oh, the anguish it brought upon Thee, good Lord! Like a sharp sword that cry pierced through Thy soul. It rang in Thy ears along the road to Calvary; wherefore Thou saidst to the daughters of Jerusalem, "Weep not for me, but weep for yourselves and for your children." It weighed upon Thy heart through all those bitter hours on the cross, when from Thy high station Thou beheldest in spirit the city doomed and desolate, and among all Thy sorrows there was not any sorrow like unto this. As each blood-drop fell to the ground, Thou knewest that it would fall upon Thy people as a curse. O merciful Jesus, by all Thy bitter sorrows, let Thy Blood be on them still, Thy precious Blood, which speaketh better things than that of Abel; let it be on them until it melt their hearts and cleanse them from their sin. And so, O Son of David, O Seed of Abraham, shall all Israel be saved. Let this be the sweet vengeance which Thou wilt take upon Thine ancient people. After much torment and many wanderings do Thou make Thyself known to them at the last, saying, "I am Joseph, your Brother. Ye thought evil against me, but God meant it unto good." As for us, wild olive trees grafted in, we would cry, O Saviour of the world, we would cry with reverent spirit, that Thy Blood be also on us and on our children, not in vengeance but in mercy, not to destroy but to save. O blessed and most salutary word, uttered at first with evil intent! We would invoke, in true faith and hearty desire, Thy Blood upon ourselves and our children for ever, to cleanse us from all defilement of body and soul. Thy Blood be on our heart and tongue, on our life and actions, to wash away all that is amiss. Purge us, good Jesus, with hyssop, and we shall be clean. Wash us, and though our sins be as scarlet, they shall be as white as snow; though they be red like crimson, they shall be as wool. Thy Blood be on us, so that when Thou shalt come at the last judgment, Thou mayest see this token and spare Thy people, that the plague come not nigh us; but that, like as Rahab escaped from death by reason of the scarlet thread hung in her window, even so we may be rescued by Thy crimson Blood from everlasting death.

III

For the Jews

O GOD, THE GOD OF ABRAHAM, look upon Thine everlasting Covenant, and cause the captivity of Judah and of Israel to return. They are Thy people, oh, be Thou their Saviour, that all who love Jerusalem, and mourn for her, may rejoice with her; for Jesus Christ's sake, their Saviour and ours. *Amen.*

For the Conversion of Israel

O SEED OF ABRAHAM, O Son of David, O Adonai and leader of the house of Israel, Who didst appear

to Moses in the burning bush, and didst on Mount
Sinai deliver to him Thy Law; O Key of David, and
sceptre of the house of Israel, Who openest and no one
shutteth, Who shuttest and no one openeth: Visit not,
O dear Lord, the sins of the fathers upon the children, continue not Thy wrath for ever, but spare this
poor nation, which was once so high in Thy sight, and
now hath fallen so low. Oh, remember not those old
Priests and Scribes, the Pharisees and Sadducees, remember not Annas and Caiaphas, Judas, and the in-
sane multitude who cried out, "Crucify Him." In wrath
remember mercy. Forgive their obstinacy and forgive
their impenitence—forgive their blindness to things
spiritual, and their avowed love of this world and its
enjoyments. Touch their hearts and give them true
faith and repentance. Have mercy, O Jesus, on Thy
own brethren—have mercy on the countrymen of Thy
Mother, of St. Joseph, of Thy Apostles, of St. Paul, of
Thy great Saints, Abraham, Moses, Samuel, David. O
Lord, hear: O Lord, be appeased: O Lord, hearken
and do; delay not for Thine own sake, O my God, for
Thy Name was once named upon the city Jerusalem
and Thy people. *Amen.*

"Let Thy Blood Be on Me"

LORD, LET THY BLOOD BE ON ME, to redeem me;
on my heart and body, to purify them; on my thoughts
and desires, to sanctify them; and on my life and actions, to consecrate them entire to Thee. *Amen.*

152

IV

"OH, THAT THE LORD'S SALVATION"

Oh, that the Lord's salvation
　　Were out of Zion come,
To heal His ancient nation,
　　To lead His outcasts home!

How long the holy city
　　Shall heathen feet profane?
Return, O Lord, in pity;
　　Rebuild her walls again.

Let fall Thy rod of terror,
　　Thy saving grace impart;
Roll back the veil of error,
　　Release the fettered heart.

Let Israel home returning,
　　Her lost Messiah see;
Give oil of joy for mourning,
　　And bind Thy Church to Thee.

✟

BLOOD OF JESUS, CLEANSE ME FROM ALL SINS

153

The Fourth Saturday

---

*I gave my back to the smiters, and my cheeks to them
that plucked off the hair: I hid my face from shame
and spitting.*

*He hath no form nor comeliness, that we should
look upon Him: nor beauty, that we should desire
Him.*

John 19:1-5

(Matt. 27:27-31; Mark 15:16-20)

Then Pilate therefore took Jesus, and scourged Him.
And the soldiers platted a crown of thorns, and put
it on His Head, and arrayed Him in a purple garment; and they came unto Him, and said, Hail, King
of the Jews! And they struck Him with their hands.
And Pilate went out again, and saith unto them,
Behold, I bring Him out to you, that ye may know
that I find no crime in Him. Jesus therefore came out,
wearing the crown of thorns and the purple garment.
And Pilate saith unto them, Behold, the Man!

I

While the other evangelists pass rapidly from the
scourging of Jesus to His crucifixion, John makes it
clear that a longer interval elapsed between the two,
and that Pilate intended the scourging to be not so
much the immediate prelude to crucifixion as a substitute for it. It was in reality his last device to secure

154

Jesus' release, as is shown by his words in Luke, "I will therefore chastise Him, and release Him."

This "chastisement" was indeed a sufficiently cruel substitute for crucifixion. Many a hardy ruffian dropped dead in his blood under the forty or more stripes, administered to bared back and breast with whips of leather cords weighted with bits of bone or metal. This brutal punishment was inflicted upon Jesus by the soldiers of the governor. And as though His cup of suffering were not full enough, to the physical pain they added the mental anguish of the mockery. They flung an old scarlet military mantle over His shoulders, pressed a crown of twisted thorns upon His head, and filing past Him in a long line, greeted Him in derisive homage, "All hail, King of the Jews!" and rained blows upon Him. Jesus was then led out, thus bruised and bleeding in body and soul, by the governor and exhibited to the people. Pilate hoped—poor psychologist, he!—that their bloodlust would be appeased by the spectacle and they would cry enough. He wished them to understand that he found nothing wrong in Jesus and that he was looking to them to consent to His release. As Jesus stepped forth and stood before them in His scarlet mantle and crown of thorns, Pilate could not forbear saying, "Behold, the man!"

It is the most enigmatic utterance of this baffling person, even more difficult to fathom than his question, "What is truth?" Undoubtedly it was a last appeal, over the heads of their own leaders, to the compassion of the crowd. At the same time there was in it a desire, not unmixed with sarcasm, to drive home to the priests and elders the absurdity of hounding so harmless a being to His death. By looking deeper, we may discern also that the Roman could not withhold a certain admiration from this Man. Pilate the governor thus takes his stand, as prophet despite himself, by the side of Caiaphas, "the high priest that same year."

II

Lord Jesus, stripped of Thy garments, bound to a pillar, and scourged by brutal soldiers! Thy visage is marred more than any man, and Thy form more than the sons of men. I shudder as the lash descends upon Thee again and yet again, drawing blood and causing unspeakable pain at every blow. Thy sacred Body is covered with wounds and bruises from head to foot. The torment is unendurable, but Thou dost think of me, and for love of me Thou dost endure it. Oh, how I love Thee for these Thy most grievous wounds! May Thy chastisement be my peace, and Thy stripes my healing. Teach me also, by Thy holy example, not to pamper nor indulge my flesh, nor to shrink back from suffering. Nay, let me buffet my body and bring it into subjection, let me make no provision for the flesh to fulfill the lusts thereof.

O Jesus, King most wonderful, I would take my place among the soldiers marching past Thee, where Thou sittest in the hall, clothed in scarlet and crowned with thorns; I would take my place among them, and coming up to Thee I would cry out most reverently, "All hail, my King!" I would kneel before Thee in unfeigned adoration, I would kiss Thy marred face, and lay my hands upon Thee in love. Give me of Thy gentleness and patience, let me never willingly inflict pain upon others nor callously witness their suffering, let me not be cruel to any living being. Grant me so to fear and love God that I may not do my neighbor any bodily harm or injury, but rather assist and comfort him in danger and want.

Open mine eyes that I may behold Thee, O Man of Sorrows, O Son of Man! Thou art the man I might have been, the Image of God in which at the beginning He made man: I behold Thee with the eyes of penitence and cry, "O wretched man that I am!" Thou art the Second Man, the Lord from heaven, the Woman's Seed that bruised the serpent's head: I behold Thee with the eyes of faith and say, "O Son of man, who wast lifted up, let me not perish, but have eternal life." Thou art the Perfect Man, the Pattern of holy manhood: I behold Thee with the eyes of love and pray, "Transform me into Thine image, let me walk in the blessed footprints of Thy most holy life, let me purify myself even as Thou art pure." Thou art that Man whom God ordained, by whom He will judge the world in righteousness: I behold Thee with the eyes of hope and plead, "O Thou who canst be touched with the feeling of our infirmities, disdain not Thy own flesh and blood, and deliver me not into the bitter pains of eternal death." Mine eyes are ever toward the Lord; for He shall pluck my feet out of the net.

"By His Stripes We Are Healed

O MAN OF SORROWS, Who for my sins wast so marred that even Thy heathen judge was moved to pity, grant me to behold Thee with the eyes of penitence and faith. Oh, let Thy stripes be my healing, Thy sacred Blood cleanse me from all sins, and Thy crown of thorns prick me in my heart, so that I may profitably contemplate Thy Passion. Let there be no condemnation to me, since I am in Thee, Christ Jesus my Saviour. *Amen.*

To Jesus Scourged

O MOST CHASTE SPOUSE, Lord Jesus Christ, very God and very Man, Who wast stripped of Thy garments, bound to a pillar, and most cruelly scourged; Who wast crowned with thorns, struck with a reed, clothed in derision with a purple garment, mocked and reviled: We implore Thee, by these Thy most grievous wounds, and by all the other torments of Thy Passion, to enable us to bear patiently whatsoever chastisements Thou mayest think fit to lay upon us, and to remember that whom the Lord loveth He chasteneth, and scourgeth every son whom He receiveth. *Amen.*

To Jesus Crowned With Thorns

O LORD JESUS CHRIST, Who wast crowned with thorns, struck with a reed, clothed in derision with a purple garment, mocked, and reviled: Have mercy on us, and pierce us so thoroughly with the thorns of penitence that we may find pardon in this life, and hereafter be found meet to be crowned by Thee with glory in Heaven. *Amen.*

IV

"SALVE CAPUT CRUENTATUM"

Hail to Thee, Thou Head of mourning!
Crowned with thorns, for pain and scorning!
Mocked and bleeding, torn and wounded,
Spat upon, with foes surrounded,
   Bruised and broken with the rod!
Hail to Thee, whose light is shrouded,
Kingly lustre overclouded;
Lo, Thy flower of beauty pining!
Thou, before whose awful shining
   Hosts of Heaven adore their God!

All Thy youth and bloom are faded:
Who hath thus Thy state degraded?
Death upon Thy face is written—
See the wan worn limbs, the smitten
   Breast upon the cruel Tree!
Thus despised and desecrated,
Thus in dying desolated;
Slain for me of sinners vilest,
Loving Lord, on me Thou smilest:
   Shine, sweet Head, and strengthen me!

In Thy Passion do not scorn me,
Gentle Shepherd, who hast borne me;
From whose mouth I drank the healing
Draught of milk and honey stealing,
   Sweeter than all sweets that be:

I am vile; yet do not spurn me!
From Thy face Thou shalt not turn me!
While the shades of death are closing,
Lean upon my breast, reposing
   Thy dear head and hands on me!

When the time is near for dying,
Listen to my lonely crying!
In that dreadful hour delay not!
Jesu, come! be quick and stay not!
   Shield me, save and set me free!
When from earth my soul is bidden,
Let not then Thy face be hidden!
Lover, whom 'tis life to cherish,
Shine and leave me not to perish!
   Show Thy Cross and succor me.

✠

LORD JESUS, MINE EYES ARE EVER TOWARD THEE

The Fourth Monday

It is better to trust in the Lord than to put confidence in man: it is better to trust in the Lord than to put confidence in princes.

Whosoever therefore will be a friend of the world: is the enemy of God.

John 19:6-16

When therefore the chief priests and the officers saw Him, they cried out, saying, Crucify Him, crucify Him! Pilate saith unto them, Take Him yourselves, and crucify Him: for I find no crime in Him. The Jews answered him, We have a law, and by that law He ought to die, because He made Himself the Son of God. When Pilate therefore heard this saying, he was the more afraid; and he entered into the Prætorium again, and saith unto Jesus, Whence art Thou? But Jesus gave him no answer. Pilate therefore saith unto Him, Speakest Thou not unto me? Knowest Thou not that I have power to release Thee, and have power to crucify Thee? Jesus answered him, Thou wouldest have no power against me, except it were given thee from above: therefore he that delivered me unto thee hath greater sin. Upon this Pilate sought to release Him: but the Jews cried out, saying, If thou release this man, thou art not Cæsar's friend: every one that maketh himself a king speaketh against Cæsar. When Pilate therefore heard these words, he brought Jesus out, and sat down on the judgment-seat at a place called the Pavement, but in Hebrew, Gabbatha. Now it was the Preparation of the passover: it was about the sixth hour. And he saith unto the Jews,

161

Behold, your King! They therefore cried out, Away
with Him, away with Him, crucify Him! Pilate saith
unto them, Shall I crucify your King? The chief
priests answered, We have no king but Cæsar. Then
therefore he delivered Him unto them to be crucified.

I

The priests and elders had succeeded in thwarting the
governor's last attempt to secure Jesus' freedom. With
their attendants they had met his "Behold, the man"
with loud shouts of "Crucify!" But their victory was
far from complete. Pilate was not yet disposed to yield,
and sarcastically bade them take Jesus and crucify
Him themselves. This left them exactly where they
had been at the beginning of the trial. They abandoned
therefore the political charge, which Pilate took so
lightly, and brought forward the religious charge, on
which they had found Jesus guilty of death. If the
governor could find no crime in Him according to
Roman law, they reminded him that the Jewish law
required this blasphemer to be put to death, and they
demanded, in accordance with Roman practice, that
their law be recognized.

This turn of events increased Pilate's perplexity by
adding a superstitious dread of his Prisoner to his fear
of the fanatical Jews. There followed a second private
interview with Jesus, in which Pilate questioned Him
about His origin, but received no reply. Incensed, he
flaunted his authority in his Prisoner's face, but was
told that whatever authority he had came from God

and carried with it a corresponding responsibility. As a result of this interview, he was more anxious than ever to release Jesus. But the priests now advanced their final argument and threatened to carry the case to the emperor along with other matters not to Pilate's credit. This threat brought the governor to his knees, for to be a "friend of Cæsar" was for him the be-all and the end-all of life. He led Jesus forth and, taking his place on the judgment-seat, formally sentenced Him to death—but not until he had sarcastically pointed Him out to the Jews as their King, and inquired if they really wished him to crucify their King. Ignoring the sarcasm and reiterating their threat, the priests replied, "We have no king but Cæsar." Then the governor pronounced sentence—"To the cross Thou shalt go!" John solemnly notes the exact hour and place at which the Jews, better Romans than the Roman, compelled the servant of Cæsar to condemn their King to the cross.

II

Consider, O my soul, the sin of Pilate, who yielded to the threat of the crafty Jews, and against his better judgment sent Jesus to the cross. Alas for human justice and honor! This sin also Thou tookest upon Thee, O Righteous Servant of the Lord. I observe in Pilate's conduct the act of a weak man enslaved by a wicked past and willing to please men rather than God. He saw through the wiles of the elders, he knew at once that their accusation was baseless, he was firmly convinced of Jesus' innocence; yet he made no determined effort to set Him free. Again and again he attempted to shift the burden of responsibility to others, he temporized, and trifled with the truth. Under such tactics the trial degenerated into a sordid conflict between Roman governor and Jewish priests, in which each side strove for the mastery from selfish motives and without regard to justice. Thus wast Thou tossed like a ball, O my good Lord, between unscrupulous opponents determined to win their own case at any cost to Thee. Oh, the indignity, the injustice, the mental anguish! And when the advantage rested on Pilate's side, and he seemed on the point of releasing Thee, up rose his evil past and bound his hands. Behind him was so unsavory a record that when the Jews threatened to carry their complaint to Rome, he gave way to fear and sacrificed all. His wrongdoing of the past unfitted him to meet the crisis of his life.

O my Lord, in what difficulties and dangers a false step in the past may involve me! Remember not against me the sins of my youth nor my transgressions: let them not have dominion over me. Let me not be hindered in my trial hour by any past wrongdoing. Yet, O good Lord, if Thou thinkest fit to plague me with old sins, give me courage to bear whatever hardship they may bring upon me; only let me not be untrue to Thee. Find me and say to me, "Sin no more, lest a worse thing come upon thee." Open my eyes to the insidious, far-reaching effects of evil-doing. I would walk to-day in Thy fear, then shall I be free to serve Thee to-morrow without fear. Thou, Lord, art plenteous in mercy, and lovest to forgive; put the sins of my past life behind Thy back, cast all my sins into the depths of the sea—far, far into the unfathomable, pardon.

Jesus, Saviour! be Thou to me the same yesterday, and to-day, and for ever.

III

The Forgiveness of Past Sins

REMIT, FORGIVE, PARDON, O Lord, all the sins of my past life, voluntary or involuntary, committed in deed, word, or thought, in ignorance or knowledge, in conception or intention (especially . . .). Forgive these and all my sins, O Lord, as Thou art good and gracious; through Jesus Christ our Lord. *Amen.*

For Those Who Are Afraid of the Opinions of Men

O GOD, THOU SEARCHER OF HEARTS, Who acceptest no man to make intercession for his brother in the day of Thy judgment: Have mercy upon those who shrink from serving Thee through consideration of human censure. Fill them with an awful sense of the implicit allegiance which they owe to Thee. Enlighten their eyes to the vanity of mere earthly opinion. Quicken within them a consciousness of Thy power to change, in whatever way Thou wilt, the purpose of those they fear. Strengthen them to bear cheerfully the reproach of the Cross. Perfect their faith; reveal to them Thy truth; kindle their zeal, that they, looking to Thee alone for success, may know what Thou requirest, and leave all consequences in Thy hands, while they accomplish Thy bidding with holy diligence; through Jesus Christ our Lord. *Amen.*

For All Rulers

O HEAVENLY FATHER, we bend the knee before Thee in behalf of all kings, princes, and governors of this world, beseeching Thee to grant unto them by Thy inspiration to rule in righteousness, to rejoice in peace, to shine in piety, and to labor for the well-being of the people committed unto them, so that by the rectitude of their government all faithful people may live without disturbance in the knowledge of Thee, and labor without hindrance for Thy glory; through Jesus Christ our Lord. *Amen.*

IV

THE DEBT

Thee, God, I come from, to Thee go,
All day long I like fountain flow
From Thy hand out, swayed about
Mote-like in Thy mighty glow.

What I know of Thee I bless,
As acknowledging Thy stress
On my being, and as seeing
Something of Thy holiness.

Once I turned from Thee and hid,
Bound on what Thou hast forbid;
Sow the wind I would: I sinned:
I repent of what I did.

166

THE FRIEND OF CÆSAR

Bad I am, but yet Thy child,
Father, be Thou reconciled.
Spare Thou me, since I see
With Thy might that Thou art mild.

I have life left with me still
And my purpose to fulfill;
Yes, a debt to pay Thee yet:
Help me, Sir, and so I will.

✠

LORD JESUS, BID ME SIN NO MORE

The Fourth Tuesday

24. SIMON OF CYRENE

I am poured out like water, and all my bones are out of joint: my heart is like wax, it is melted in the midst of my bowels.

I will declare Thy name unto my brethren: in the midst of the congregation will I praise Thee.

Mark 15:20-21

(Matt. 27:32; Luke 23:26).

And they compel one passing by, Simon of Cyrene, coming from the country, the father of Alexander and Rufus, to go with them, that he might bear His cross.

I

During each passover the holy city was crowded with hundreds of thousands of festival pilgrims, not only from every part of Palestine, but from all parts of the world. Despite the hospitality of the people of Jerusalem, there was not nearly enough room for them all within the city. Many had to find lodging in near-by villages, others were obliged to tent out in the open country. Among these was Simon, a man from Cyrene in North Africa.

After spending the night outside the walls he was on his way to the city, in order to worship in the temple or perhaps to visit friends. As he was about to pass through the city gate, he found his way barred by the mournful procession bound for Calvary. The long line halted, for one of the criminals had fallen under the weight of His cross. Simon pressed closer to see. The man looked utterly spent, scarce able to drag Himself along, let alone the heavy beam. In a moment Simon regretted his curiosity. A soldier leaped forward, grasped him roughly by the arm, and ordered him to carry the man's cross for Him. He dared not refuse, for he had been officially pressed into service; but his face burned with anger and shame. What a misfortune! Why had he not set out a few minutes sooner or later? What would his friends say if they saw him? To march at the head of the long procession, on this festival day, staggering under a cross like any criminal, surrounded by the taunts of the soldiers glad of an opportunity to bait the Jew—surely this passover Simon would not forget until his dying day!

Thus we may picture the scene and imagine the thoughts that passed through Simon's mind. That is all we know about him, except the little notice that Mark appends to his name, designating him as the father of Alexander and Rufus. From this we conjecture that these two men were well known figures, and probably members, in the early Christian community in which our second gospel originated. We may suppose also that Simon and his sons became believers as a result of that Good Friday experience. Precisely when the turning point came in Simon's life—whether that day, or shortly afterwards, or not until years later—we cannot tell. All we are sure of is that when Mark wrote his gospel, the two sons were well known Christians. The shame of the father had become the glory of the children. Thus Jesus repaid even an unwilling act of kindness shown Him in His hour of need.

II

Good Jesus, I rejoice at the solace offered to Thee on Thy Painful Way, though it was but the bearing of Thy gallows tree to the place of execution. Ah, how the burden of our sins pressed upon Thee and crushed Thee to the ground! Blessed be Simon, who bore for Thee the heavy cross! As I look upon him toiling by Thy side, and covet the privilege that was his, I hear Thee say, "If any man will come after me, let him deny himself, and take up his cross, and follow me." O Lord, I am Thy servant; give me understanding, that I may know Thy testimonies. I know that the cross Thou dost bid me take up is not Thy Cross. That burden is not for me; it has been borne once for all, first by Thee and then by Simon, and on it Thou hast borne our sins in Thine own body. It need not and cannot be borne again. Nor is my cross any deserved pain or trouble, which I have brought upon myself by folly or wrongdoing; as St. Peter saith, "Let none of you suffer as a murderer, or as a thief, or as an evildoer." Nay, my cross is the suffering that befalls me in my Christian course, any reproach or loss that I must endure for Thy sake and the Gospel's; as St. Peter saith again, "If any man suffer as a Christian, let him not be ashamed; but let him glorify God on this behalf." O my Lord, I am ashamed to call even such suffering a cross; it is not fit to be mentioned in the same breath with Thy Cross, it is not deserving of the name. Yet Thou Thyself hast graciously given it this name. Thus art Thou pleased to hallow and sanctify to me my sorrows and enable me to glory in my tribulation, seeing I am permitted not only to believe in Thee, but also to suffer for Thy sake.

My cross, then, O sweet Saviour, is not Thine, but mine. And yet it is Thine, for it comes from Thee and is intended to lead to Thee. Nevertheless, it is not Thine, but mine. Behold now, I have taken upon me to speak unto the Lord, which am but dust and ashes. Bear with me, and enlighten me by Thy Word. My cross, I say, is not Thine, but mine. For Thou hast chosen it for me and hast laid it upon me. It is mine, and no one else's; it belongs to me, even as my name, my body, or mind, or any of my personal possessions. Then it can never be too heavy for me, as Thy Cross was for Thee. Thy Cross was too heavy for Thee because it was not Thine, but mine and all the world's. My cross is mine alone, and Thine only as Thou wilt help me bear it. For since it comes from Thee and must needs be borne after Thee, Thou wilt help me bear it, even as Simon helped Thee. O little cross of mine! most true Relic, most precious Jewel! let me embrace thee, let me take thee up, let me bear thee after my crucified Lord.

III

A SHORT LITANY OF THE CROSS

Lord, have mercy.
Christ, have mercy.
Lord, have mercy.

O Lord Jesus Christ, Lamb of God, That takest away the
sins of the world,
Have mercy upon us, and forgive us our sins.

Jesus, Who camest to seek and to save that which was lost,
Have mercy upon us, and forgive us our sins.

Jesus, the Propitiation for our sins,
Have mercy upon us, and forgive us our sins.

By Thy Life of toil,
Pity and sustain us.

By Thy Victory in temptation,
Succor us in our trials.

By Thy Watchings and Prayers,
Uphold our weary spirits when we would watch with Thee.

By Thy Carrying Thy Cross to Calvary,
Give us grace to bear our little cross in patience after Thee.

By all Thine unknown sorrows,
Have compassion upon us.

OUR FATHER.

For Self-denial

ALMIGHTY GOD, Whose beloved Son Jesus Christ
for us men and for our salvation endured the Cross,
despising the shame: Grant that, always looking to
Him, I may have grace to crucify this sinful flesh with
the affections and lusts, and taking up my cross daily
may follow after Him, until I attain to the place where
He now is set down at the right hand of Thy throne

on high; through the same Jesus Christ our Lord. *Amen.*

That We May Not Fall

O JESUS, Who for our sins didst bear the heavy burden of the Cross and didst fall under the weight, may the thought of Thy sufferings make us watchful against temptation, and do Thou stretch out Thy sacred Hand to help us lest we fall into any grievous sin. *Amen.*

IV

THE HIGHWAY TO CALVARY

So from Jerusalem
The soul's Physician goes,
When they forsook His saving health,
And vowed themselves His foes.

Behold what multitudes
Do guard thy God about
Who bleeding bears His dying Tree
Amidst the Jewish rout:

Centurion hard at hand,
The thieves upon the side,
The exclamations, shouts and cries,
The shame He doth abide.

Then press amongst the throng,
Thy self in sorrow's weed;
Get very near to Christ, and see
What tears the women shed.

Then look toward Jesus' load,
More than He could endure,
And how for help to bear the same
A hireling they procure.

Join thou unto the Cross;
Bear it of love's desire;
Do not as Cyrenaeus did,
That took it up for hire.

It is a grateful deed
If willing underta'en;
But if compulsion set a-work,
The labor's done in vain.

Up to Mount Calvary
If thou desir'st to go,
Then take thy cross, and follow Christ,
Thou canst not miss it so.

✠

O GOD OF THE CROSSES THAT ARE LAID UPON US,
HELP THY SERVANT

The Fifth Wednesday

25. THE WEEPING DAUGHTERS OF JERUSALEM

Arise, O Jerusalem, and put off thy garments of joy: put on ashes and sackcloth.

Shed thy tears like a torrent, day and night: and let not the apple of thine eye be dry.

Luke 23:27-31

And there followed Him a great multitude of the people, and of women who bewailed and lamented Him. But Jesus turning unto them said, Daughters of Jerusalem, weep not for me, but weep for yourselves, and for your children. For behold, the days are coming, in which they shall say, Blessed are the barren, and the wombs that never bare, and the breasts that never gave suck. Then shall they begin to say to the mountains, Fall on us; and to the hills, Cover us. For if they do these things in the green tree, what shall be done in the dry?

I

In the throng accompanying our Lord to Calvary were many women of Jerusalem, who beat their breasts and loudly lamented Him, going in the flower of manhood to His death. Though He was not ungrateful for their sympathy, He bade them save their pity for themselves. However dreadful His way, it was the way of the righteous, which the Lord knoweth; they were all unwittingly in the way of the ungodly, which shall perish.

175

If these daughters of doomed Jerusalem could behold the city as Jesus beheld it, they would weep for themselves and for their children, as He had wept but a few days before. Again the vision rose before His eyes —Jerusalem besieged on every side and laid even with the ground, not one stone left upon another, and her little ones dashed against the rock. Above the weeping of the women there rang in His ears the terrible cry of their husbands and fathers, the cause of all that woe—"His blood be on us, and on our children."

Even now, in His rejection, that dreadful doom was gathering. If this was what happened when the wood was green, what would happen when the wood was dry? If the righteous scarcely should be saved, where would the ungodly and the sinner appear? Of Jesus it has been said, "Blessed is the womb that bare Thee, and the breasts which Thou didst suck"; but in those days the cry would be, "Blessed are the barren, and the wombs that never bare, and the breasts that never gave suck." The destruction of Jerusalem was but a figure and foretaste of the end of all, when men would seek death and not find it, when they would call in vain upon hills and mountains to hide them from the wrath to come.

Jesus, therefore, forgetting His own sorrows, tenderly charged the daughters of Jerusalem to weep for themselves and for their children. It was especially the fate of the children that weighed upon His soul. If these mothers would rend their hearts and not their garments, and turn to the Lord their God, who could tell but He might return and repent, and leave a blessing behind? Perhaps He would say, as He said to Jonah, "Should I not spare this great city, wherein there are so many thousands that cannot discern between their right hand and their left?" Jesus, greater than Jonah, would not grieve or sulk, if his prediction were not fulfilled. Alas! there seemed but little likelihood of that default. The things that belonged to Jerusalem's peace were hidden from her eyes, she knew not the time of her visitation. Hence the tears and lamentations of the women only added to Jesus' sufferings on His Way to the Cross; He heard in them the weeping and wailing when His blood would come in vengeance on His faithless people.

II

Good Jesus, bearing Thy Cross to Calvary, Thou art the Friend of children even unto death. Thy heart was pierced with pity for them, when Thou saidst to the weeping mothers, "Weep for yourselves and for your children." Be with me, O Lover of childlike souls, while I meditate on the place of these little ones in Thy Holy Passion. That fairest scene in the gospels —my Lord the centre of a group of young children— does it not belong in the time of Thy suffering and form one of the earliest incidents of the Painful Way? Thou hadst set Thy face to go to Jerusalem, thoughts of suffering and death filled Thy mind, when these little ones waylaid Thee and made Thee smile. Thy foes were plotting against Thee, Thou wast rejected by Thy people, and misunderstood by Thy disciples; but these tiny folk did not reject Thee, instinctively they understood Thee, they were Thy friends. Joyfully didst Thou gather them to Thy heart, put Thy hands upon them, and bless them. In them Thou heldest the future in Thine arms.

Again, when Thou hadst entered the city, Thy way spread with green branches and loud with psalms, a troop of merry children met Thee in the temple, and imitating their elders, ran after Thee, crying, "Hosanna!" Did not their childish voices sound more sweetly in Thine ears than the shouts of the multitude? Verily, it was for Thee the perfection of praise. At least, these simple hosannas did not turn to "crucify."

No wonder, then, Good Jesus, that Thou hadst the children in mind on the road to Calvary, and thinking of Thy people's woe Thou didst think first of them. Thou didst carry them in Thy heart when Thou ascendedst the Cross. And Thou didst not forget them when, after the Resurrection, Thou sentest forth Thy followers to make disciples of all the nations by baptizing and by teaching. Fittingly, therefore, do we trace the sign of the Cross upon their brows in Holy Baptism, in token that they are Thy very own, pledged to walk from their earliest footsteps after the Captain of our salvation. Let men beware of causing one of these little ones to stumble. Let parents and sponsors faithfully bring them up in the nurture and admonition of the Lord. Yea, let us all become even as little children, that so we may enter with them into the kingdom of God.

III

For Grafting in the Green Tree Christ

O LORD JESUS CHRIST, Thou green and living Tree, grant that we, who are by nature dry and unfruitful branches, may be grafted by true faith in Thee, that so we may draw from Thee strength and nourishment to bring forth fruit that abideth for ever. *Amen.*

For Godly Weeping

O LORD JESUS, we mourn and will mourn both for Thee and for ourselves; for Thy sufferings, and for our sins which caused them. Oh, teach us so to mourn, that we may be comforted, and escape those dreadful judgments prepared for all those who reject and neglect Thee. *Amen.*

O GOD OF INFINITE MERCY! I grieve for love of Thee, and am heartily sorry that I have ever sinned against Thee. I love Thee with my whole heart; may I never again offend Thee. Oh, may I love Thee without ceasing, and delight in all things to do Thy holy will. *Amen.*

For Our Children at Home

ALMIGHTY GOD and heavenly Father, we thank Thee for the children Thou hast given us: give us also grace to train them in Thy faith, fear, and love, that as they advance in years they may grow in grace, and may hereafter be found in the number of Thine elect; through Jesus Christ our Lord. *Amen.*

At School

ALMIGHTY GOD, Who hast promised that Thy holy city Jerusalem shall be full of boys and girls playing in the streets thereof: Give Thy sure protection to our school-children, as in their prayers and studies, so in their sports and exercise. Make them chaste and strong, brave and gentle, loving and obedient; that, bringing their bodies into subjection, and with Thy holy angels to shield them, they may obtain not only earthly rewards, but eternal blessings; through Jesus Christ our Lord. *Amen.*

IV

"WEINT NICHT UEBER JESU SCHMERZEN"

Wherefore weep we over Jesus,
    O'er His death and bitter smart?
Weep we rather that He sees us
    Unconvinced and hard of heart;
For His soul was never tainted
    With the smallest spot or stain:
'Twas for us He was acquainted
    With such depths of grief and pain.

Oh! what profits it with groaning
    Underneath His Cross to stand;
Oh! what profits our bemoaning
    His pale brow and bleeding hand?
Wherefore gaze on Him expiring,
    Railed at, pierced, and crucified,

180

While we think not of inquiring
    Wherefore and for whom He died?

And for whom hath He contended
    In a strife so strange and new?
And for whom to hell descended?
    Brothers! 'twas for me and you!
Now you see that He was reaping
    Punishment for us alone;
And we have good cause for weeping,
    Not for His guilt, but our own.

If we then make full confession,
    Joined with penitence and prayer,
If we see our own transgression
    In the punishment He bare,
If we mourn with true repentance,
    We shall hear the Saviour say,
"Fear not: I have borne your sentence;
    Wipe your bitter tears away."

✠

RIVERS OF WATERS RUN DOWN MINE EYES,

BECAUSE THEY KEEP NOT THY LAW

The Fifth Thursday

26. CRUCIFIXION

They pierced my hands and my feet: I may tell all my bones: they look and stare upon me.
   They part my garments among them: and cast lots upon my vesture.

Mark 15:22-25

(Matt. 27:33-35; Luke 23:33; John 19:17-18)

And they bring Him unto the place Golgotha, which is, being interpreted, The place of a skull. And they offered Him wine mingled with myrrh: but he received it not. And they crucify Him, and part His garments among them, casting lots upon them, what each should take. And it was the third hour, and they crucified Him.

I

The procession arrived finally at The Skull, as the place of execution was called, probably from its skull-like contour. Despite the assistance of His cross-bearer, Jesus was so weak that He must be helped up the hill; the rough soldiers were obliged to put their arms round Him and lead Him, as one leads a sick person or a young child. According to a humane custom, drugged wine, furnished by charitable women of Jerusalem, was administered before crucifixion, in order that the criminals might "remember their misery no more."

This potion was offered to Jesus, but after putting His lips to it He refused to drink. He would taste death for us with every sense alert and render up His soul to God unclouded.

> I would hate that death bandaged my eyes and forbore,
> And bade me creep past.

It was well for the penitent robber, and not for him alone, that Jesus did not drink the wine.

The cross had been taken from Simon's shoulders and placed flat upon the ground. Jesus was now stripped of His clothing and laid upon it. Quietly and making no resistance, He let the soldiers have their will. Nay, of His own accord and with great willingness, He sat down and stretched His body upon the long beam, extending His arms to either side and placing His feet in the right position. The soldiers grasped hammer and nails, and pierced His right hand and His left, and both feet. The cross was raised and set down with a shock into the opening prepared for it, where it was propped and fastened. The shame of crucifixion was as keen a torment for Jesus' soul as the pain was for His body. Naked as He had come from God He went to God, taking with Him nothing that was man's but his sin. The soldiers, after completing their bloody work, sat under the cross distributing His clothes among themselves by drawing lots.

II

Sacred Hands of Jesus, nailed fast to the Cross! Hands of the Carpenter, hardened with toil; Hands of the

Miracle-worker, healing the sick, multiplying the loaves, waking the dead maiden; strong Hands, swinging the scourge and cleansing the Father's house; gentle Hands, laid in blessing on little children's heads; holy Hands, lifted in prayer to God! Bleeding Hands, bound with cords and pierced with nails! I grieve for whatever evil I have by my hands committed, for whatever good I have left undone. O Hands, spread out all day upon the Cross, inviting the weary and heavy laden! I would come to you and find rest unto my soul. I would get me strength to work henceforth with my hands the thing which is good, that I may have to give to him that needeth.

Sacred Feet, beautiful upon the mountain, of Him that bringeth peace! Tireless Feet, on which He went about doing good; Feet at which Mary sat hearing His word and which she anointed with precious nard, which the great sinner washed with her tears and wiped with her hair, at which Jairus and the Syrophenician lay asking mercy, and the cleansed Samaritan giving thanks! Bleeding Feet, which found the way to Calvary and were nailed to the Cross! I kneel before you in grief and shame for the swiftness of my feet to evil, their slowness on errands of love. I who have not kept my feet when I went to the house of God, who have passed by my neighbor on the other side, run to you for pardon and for strength to follow in your footprints, for grace to visit the fatherless and widows, the sick and imprisoned, and to **keep myself** unspotted from the world.

Good Jesus, stripped of Thy raiment and hanging naked on the Tree! grant me the seamless robe of Thy righteousness, to clothe me from head to foot, to hide my transgression and cover my sin, that the shame of my nakedness do not appear. Let it be my coat of many colors, stained with Thy blood, the token of the Father's favor; my working dress in Thy Vineyard, my wedding garment at Thy Feast.

O Saviour of the world, Who by Thy Cross and precious Blood hast redeemed us, save us and help us, we humbly beseech Thee, O Lord.

III

For the Blessing of the Crucified

O LORD JESUS CHRIST, Who hanging on the Tree wast made a curse for us, grant us to be partakers of Thy heavenly blessing. O Thou Who wast wounded for our transgressions and bruised for our iniquities, let Thy precious Blood flow down upon us, to cleanse us from our sins and strengthen us unto life eternal. *Amen.*

For Fear and Love of Christ Crucified

O JESUS! MAKER OF THE WORLD, Whom no measure can mete nor bound contain, Who holdest the earth within the hollow of Thy hand: Call to mind the anguish of Thy torment, when the soldiers first fastened Thy most holy hands with blunt nails to the

Cross, and added agony to agony to Thy wounds, when to fit Thy Body for their purpose and drive the nails through Thy tender feet, they wrenched Thee so upon the Cross's length and breadth, that all Thy limbs were out of joint. I implore Thee by the memory of Thy Cross's hallowed and most bitter anguish, make me fear Thee, make me love Thee. *Amen.*

For Perfect Obedience

O MOST BLESSED, most gracious Saviour Jesus, Who by Thy obedience unto death, even the death of the Cross, didst become the Sacrifice of the world, the great Example of patience, the Lord of life, the good Shepherd laying down Thy life for the sheep, and the one Mediator between God and man: Let Thy wounds heal me, Thy Blood cleanse me, Thy death make me to live, and Thy Spirit make me to work righteousness all my days; that by Thy aid, and after Thy example, I may obey my heavenly Father with all my powers and all my faculties, with my reason and my affections, with my soul and with my body, with my time and with my substance, in prosperity and adversity; that I may bear my cross patiently, and do Thy work cheerfully in my vocation and ministry, to Thy glory and the benefit of my neighbor; that so, being a follower of Thy life and a partaker of Thy death, I may receive a part in the resurrection of the just, and enter into the joys of God in Thy inheritance, O most blessed, most gracious Saviour Jesus. *Amen.*

IV

CRUCIFIXION

"Fill high the bowl, and spice it well, and pour
The dews oblivious: for the cross is sharp,
  The cross is sharp, and He
  Is tenderer than a lamb.

"He wept by Lazarus' grave—how will He bear
This bed of anguish?—and His pale weak form
  Is worn with many a watch
  Of sorrow and unrest.

"His sweat last night was as great drops of blood;
And the sad burthen pressed Him so to earth
  The very torturers paused
  To help Him on His way.

"Fill high the bowl, benumb His aching sense
With medicined sleep."—Oh, awful in Thy woe!
  The parching thirst of death
  Is on Thee, and Thou triest

The slumberous potion bland, and wilt not drink:
Not sullen, nor in scorn, like haughty man
  With suicidal hand
  Putting his solace by:

But as at first Thine all-pervading look
Saw from Thy Father's bosom to the abyss,
  Measuring in calm presage
  The infinite descent;

So to the end, though now of mortal pangs
Made heir, and emptied of Thy glory awhile,
  With unaverted eye
  Thou meetest all the storm.

✠

LORD JESUS, LET ME KNOW NOTHING SAVE THEE CRUCIFIED

The Fifth Friday

27. THE FIRST WORD ON THE CROSS

He hath poured out His soul unto death: and He was numbered with the transgressors.

And He bare the sins of many: and made intercession for the transgressors.

Luke 23:34

And Jesus said, Father, forgive them; for they know not what they do.

I

The Passion of our Lord is not a pantomime, or mute spectacle, which we are left to interpret for ourselves. Accompanying the sufferings are the words of the Sufferer, in which their meaning is made known. As His death is the crown of His life, so His dying utterances are the crown and flower of all His sayings. The Seven Words on the Cross are the revelation of the inmost heart of the Saviour in the act and agony of His saving work.

The First Word was spoken after the cross had been raised and made fast.

"Father," He said, not "God." It was His invariable approach with all cheerfulness and confidence, the note on which His life began and ended. He was not therefore, addressing an angry God thirsting for human blood. "God was in Christ," says Paul, "reconciling the world unto Himself." It was the Father's business that Jesus was about, now as always. Never, indeed, was the Father more truly His Father than now, when both of them together were carrying out in time and space their eternal counsel of salvation.

"Father, forgive," He said, expressing the Father's purpose in coming into the world, now being fulfilled in His death. It was the voice of the whole Passion in its relation to God, the translation into words of that which was here taking place—the united act of the Father and the Son whereby the holy love of God met the sin of man, and remained holy as well as love.

"Father," He said, "forgive them," not "forgive me." Here is the strongest evidence of Jesus' sinlessness. In the hour of death a man's life passes before him, and his faults weigh heavily on his heart, so that he dare not go to meet his Maker without a prayer for pardon. Yet Jesus, in His dying hour, craved no forgiveness for Himself, but only for others. Truly, He knew no sin. The forgiveness He asked was for His executioners, His judges, His betrayer, His people, all men whose sins He was bearing on the Tree.

"They do not know," He said, "what they are doing." How could they understand the secret counsel of eternity here being carried to completion, that loving pact whereby Jesus and the Father planned to conquer sin by means of this most grievous sin of all? Thus His love found an excuse for His brethren and covered the multitude of their sins.

Jesus' prayer was answered three days later, when He that was delivered for our offences was raised again for our justification. It is answered again and again, whenever the Father sees, a great way off, a son of His returning, has compassion, and runs, and falls on his neck, and kisses him.

II

O man, forgive thy mortal foe,
Nor ever strike him blow for blow;
For all the souls on earth that live
To be forgiven must forgive.
Forgive him seventy times and seven:
For all the blessed souls in Heaven
Are both forgivers and forgiven!

O most merciful Saviour, praying in the sharpness of death for Thy murderers! I kneel before Thy Cross and long for a place in this Thy prayer. Was not this most sweet intercession spoken also for me? Thou didst pray for all, as many as by their sins had brought Thee to the Cross. Thou didst pray for the soldiers who with their own hands crucified Thee; for Pilate who sentenced Thee to death; for the rabble that shouted "crucify"; for the men who scourged Thee and crowned Thee with thorns, who mocked Thee and spit upon Thy face. Thou didst pray for Herod who with his troops set Thee at nought; for those wicked priests Annas and Caiaphas, and all that Council that found Thee guilty of death; for Judas who betrayed Thee, Peter who denied Thee, and the others who forsook Thee. Thou didst pray for Thy people who disowned Thee, yea, for all sinners didst Thou pray, back to Adam who was the first cause of the sin Thou hadst to bear. Thou didst pray for all, as many as Thou wast shedding Thy blood for; and verily, Thou gavest Thyself a ransom for all. O good Jesus, gracious Jesus, forasmuch as Thou hast said, "Father, forgive them," we, too, may say, "Father, forgive us"; for now Thy Father is our Father, and Thy God our God.

Most holy Redeemer, be Thou also My Pattern of intercession. Teach me, by Thy First Word of the Cross, to pray for my enemies, loving them even as Thou hast loved me. When Thou wast reviled, Thou reviledst not again; when Thou sufferedst, Thou threatenedst not; but didst commit Thyself to Him that judgeth righteously. Thus Thou didst commend on Mount Calvary Thy words spoken in the Mount of Blessings —"Love your enemies, do good to them that hate you, bless them that curse you, pray for them that despite-fully use you." It is a good thing to call upon Thee in time of trouble; it is better to come before Thee in unselfish intercession for my brethren; it is best of all, because likest Thee, to pray for my enemies. Let this be the revenge I take upon them—in love to plot against them in the secret place of prayer, to heap on their heads coals of fire from my altar of intercession. Let me pray for the brother who hath aught against me, before I go to be reconciled to him; so shall I marvel at the softening of his heart. Even so, Lord Jesus, Thou didst pray for them that crucified Thee, and lo! before the sun went down, the centurion acknowledged Thee to be the Son of God.

III

The First Word

We adore Thee, O Christ, and we bless Thee,
Because by Thy Cross and precious Blood Thou hast redeemed the world.

O MOST BELOVED LORD JESUS CHRIST, Who for love of me didst suffer agonies on the Cross, that Thou mightest by Thy sufferings pay the debt of my sins; and even in that hour of Thy Passion didst pray for my pardon from God's eternal justice: Have mercy on all Christians in the hour of death, and on me in my last agony. Through the merits of Thy most precious Blood, shed for our salvation, give me a true and deep sorrow for my sins, and grant that at the hour of my death I may in peace and confidence breathe out my soul into the bosom of Thine infinite mercy. *Amen.*

OUR FATHER

GLORY BE TO THE FATHER.

Have mercy on us, O Lord,
Have mercy on us.

O my God, I believe in Thee, I hope in Thee, I love Thee, and I grieve that I have so often wounded Thee by my sins.

For the Pardon for Which Jesus Prayed

O JESUS! HEAVENLY PHYSICIAN, call to mind the languor, the bruises, and the pain which, uplifted on the Cross, Thou sufferedst in all Thy rended limbs, when all were wrenched asunder, and from the sole of the foot unto the head there was no whole part in Thee, and no sorrow could be found like unto Thy sorrow; and yet, wholly unmindful of all Thy griefs, Thou didst pray the Father for Thine enemies, and saidst so lovingly, "Father, forgive them, for they know not what they do."

By this Thy mercy, by the memory of Thy sorrow, grant me that this remembrance of Thy most bitter Passion may be the full remission of all my sins. *Amen.*

A Prayer to Christ for My Enemies

Lord jesus christ, Lord of all power and goodness, Who alone art almighty, whatsoever Thou makest me to desire for mine enemies, be that Thy gift unto them, and Thine answer to my prayer. If I at any time ask for them anything that transgresseth the rule of love, whether through ignorance or infirmity or through wickedness, neither do that to them, nor fulfill my petition therein. Thou Who art the true Light, enlighten their blindness. Thou Who art supreme Truth, amend their error. Thou Who art the true Life, quicken their souls. This is the vengeance which my inmost heart desireth to ask of Thee upon my fellow servants, mine enemies and fellow sinners. This is the punishment which my soul asketh upon them—that they should love Thee and one another, according to Thy will and as is expedient for us, so that we may satisfy our common Master and serve our common Lord. This vengeance I, Thy sinful servant, pray may be prepared against all those that wish me evil and do me evil. Do Thou prepare this also, most merciful Lord, against Thy sinful servant likewise. Hear me not according to the desires of my heart or the requests of my lips, but as Thou knowest and willest that I ought to will and ask, O Saviour of the world, Who with the Father and the Holy Ghost livest and reignest God, world without end. *Amen.*

IV

"JESUS, IN THY DYING WOES"

Jesus, in Thy dying woes,
Even while Thy life-blood flows,
Craving pardon for Thy foes:
    Hear us, Holy Jesus.

Saviour, for our pardon sue,
When our sins Thy pangs renew,
For we know not what we do:
    Hear us, Holy Jesus.

O may we, who mercy need,
Be like Thee in heart and deed,
When with wrong our spirits bleed:
    Hear us, Holy Jesus.

✠

O JESUS, LET ME BE BOTH FORGIVEN AND FORGIVING

The Fifth Saturday

28. I. N. R. I.

The Lord shall send the rod of Thy strength out of Zion: rule Thou in the midst of Thine enemies.
Be Thou exalted, O God, above the heavens: and Thy glory above the earth.

John 19:19-22

(Matt. 27:37; Mark 15:26; Luke 23:38)

And Pilate wrote a title also, and put it on the cross. And there was written, Jesus of Nazareth, the King of the Jews. This title therefore read many of the Jews, for the place where Jesus was crucified was nigh to the city; and it was written in Hebrew, and in Latin, and in Greek. The chief priests of the Jews therefore said to Pilate, Write not, The King of the Jews; but, that He said, I am the King of the Jews. Pilate answered, What I have written I have written.

I

It was customary to affix to the cross, above the criminal's head, a title publishing his crime, as a warning to others. The title on Jesus' cross was intended to serve the further purpose of vexing and humiliating the Jewish leaders. The taunt, "Behold, your King!" which they had been compelled to hear from Pilate's lips at Gabbatha, they must see before them in written form on Calvary—

JESUS OF NAZARETH
KING OF THE JEWS

195

Not they alone, but every passer-by must see it; and since the place of execution was not far from the city, there was soon a throng present, of both native Jews and festival pilgrims. Moreover, all that saw the inscription were able to read it, for it was written in three languages—Hebrew, or Aramaic, the folk tongue of Palestine; Latin, the official language of the Roman empire; and Greek, the speech of the civilized world.

Here was a serious blow to priests and elders, which threatened to spoil their enjoyment of the day. A committee waited on Pilate, therefore, with the request that the objectionable title be changed. The fact it set forth was undeniable; it was the charge they themselves had laid before the governor. What they suggested was that it be put, as it were, in quotation marks. Instead of "The King of the Jews," they wished him to write, "He said, 'I am the King of the Jews.' "

But Pilate, who had yielded so much, was suddenly firm and refused point blank to alter a word. "What I have written," he said, "I have written"—another of his sayings that meant so much more than he knew. Thus the title hung all day, unchanged, above Jesus' head, with its message of glory and of shame.

II

In three languages, O Jesus, King of the Jews, the title on Thy Cross announces the shame of Thy people, the glory of their King, and the worldwide destiny of Thy kingdom.

The Hebrew sets forth, in their own language, the shame of Thy people Israel. In the days of Thy holy infancy wise men came from the East to Jerusalem, asking, "Where is the King of the Jews?" Could they return this day, and take the road to Calvary, and read the title hanging like a baleful star above Thy head, they would find their question answered, "This is the King of the Jews." Here hangs the Son of God, the King of Israel, crucified by the Romans at His people's bidding! No wonder the priests chafed at this placarding of their shame and sought to have it changed.

The Latin publishes Thy glory, O wondrous King, Thy excellent Name in all the earth. Though Pilate wrote it in mockery, it expresses an eternal and divine truth. What he had written at the dictation of God, whose word shall not return unto Him void, but shall accomplish that which He pleases and prosper in the thing whereto He sent it. "Yet have I set my King upon my holy hill." Do what they will, they cannot unking Thee. Right royally Thou wearest Thy crown of thorns; Thou ascendest the cross and it becomes a throne; Thy Blood covers Thee as a kingly and purple robe. Thou rulest in the midst of Thine enemies; Thou reignest from the Tree.

The Greek proclaims the worldwide reach of Thy kingdom. Let the Jews cast Thee out, Thou goest to the Gentiles. A little while and Thou wilt send forth Thy apostles into all the world, to preach the Gospel to every creature, to make disciples of all the nations. Thy kingdom shall have no end. Thou wilt pour out Thy Spirit upon all flesh, and dwellers in far-off lands shall hear, every man in his own tongue, the wonderful works of God. They shall speak of the glory of Thy Kingdom, and talk of Thy power; to make known to the sons of men Thy mighty acts, and the glorious majesty of Thy kingdom. Thy kingdom is an everlasting kingdom, and Thy dominion endureth throughout all generations. At Thy Name, O Jesus, every knee shall bow, and every tongue shall confess that Thou art Lord, to the glory of God the Father.

I will extol Thee, my God, O King; and I will bless Thy Name for ever and ever.

III

"My King and My God"

O LORD JESUS CHRIST, declared by the title on Thy Cross to be Jesus, the King of the Jews, be Thou my Jesus and Saviour, my King and my God. Preserve me in Thy Kingdom of grace, and receive me into Thy Kingdom of Glory. Let Thy poverty enrich my soul, and Thy nakedness clothe me, that my shame appear not before the eyes of Thy Father in heaven. *Amen.*

A Pleading for Unbelievers

O CHRIST, Who didst leave the synagogue on account of its incredulity, and didst gather together Thy Church out of an innumerable company of all nations, thus accomplishing the prophecy that all the ends of the earth shall remember themselves and be turned to the Lord, and all the kindreds of the nations shall worship before Him: Raise up children of belief from the circumcision, that they who come may be received to the kingdom of faith, and that they who have been received may not, through any sin, be deprived of Thine heritage. *Amen*. Through Thy mercy, O our God, Who art blessed, and livest and governest all things, to ages of ages. *Amen*.

That I May Live Under Christ in His Kingdom

O JESUS CHRIST, true God, begotten of the Father from eternity, and also true Man, born of the Virgin Mary, Who art my Lord, and hast redeemed me, a lost and condemned creature, secured and delivered me from all sins, from death, and from the power of the devil, not with silver and gold, but with Thy holy and precious Blood and with Thine innocent sufferings and death: Grant that I may be Thine own, live under Thee in Thy kingdom, and serve Thee in everlasting righteousness, innocence, and blessedness; even as Thou art risen from the dead, and livest and reignest to all eternity. *Amen*.

IV

"VEXILLA REGIS PRODEUNT"

The royal banners forward go,
The Cross shines forth in mystic glow,
Where He in flesh, our flesh Who made,
Our sentence bore, our ransom paid.

Fulfilled is now what David told
In true prophetic song of old,
How God the heathen's King should be,
For God is reigning from the Tree.

199

THE MAN OF SORROWS

O Tree of glory, Tree most fair,
Ordained those holy limbs to bear,
How bright in purple robe it stood,
The purple of a Saviour's blood!

Upon its arms, like balance true,
He weighed the price for sinners due,
The price which none but He could pay,
And spoiled the spoiler of his prey.

To Thee, eternal Three in One,
Let homage meet by all be done:
As by the Cross Thou dost restore,
So rule and guide us evermore.

✠

THOU ART THE KING OF GLORY, O CHRIST

The Fifth Monday

---

*All they that see me laugh me to scorn: they shoot
out the lip, they shake the head, saying,*

*He trusted on the Lord, that He would deliver
Him: let Him deliver Him, seeing He delighted in
Him.*

Mark 15:27-32

(Matt. 27:38-44; Luke 23:35-37)

And with Him they crucify two robbers; one on His
right hand, and one on His left. And they that passed
by railed on Him, wagging their heads, and saying,
Ha! Thou that destroyest the temple, and buildest it
in three days, save Thyself, and come down from
the cross. In like manner also the chief priests mocking
Him among themselves with the scribes said, He saved
others; Himself He cannot save. Let the Christ, the
King of Israel, now come down from the cross, that
we may see and believe. And they that were crucified
with Him reproached Him.

I

The title on the cross, intended by Pilate as a final
insult to the Jews, drew down upon our Lord a storm
of abuse and blasphemy from the soldiers, the populace,
the elders, and the crucified robbers.

The designation of Jesus as King of the Jews
prompted the soldiers, under the direction of the cen-

turion, to give to His cross the place of honor between those of the two robbers. Thus He was not only numbered with the transgressors, but singled out as Archtransgressor. Afterwards, as Luke reports, the soldiers mocked Him by coming up to His cross, offering Him vinegar, and saying, "If you are the King of the Jews, save yourself."

The passers-by stopped to spell out the inscription and then heap insults upon this sorry King. Someone in the crowd told about the testimony at the trial the night before, and it seemed a fine jest with which to taunt the Sufferer. "Ha!" they cried, nodding their heads in derision, "you are the man who was going to tear down the temple and build it in three days. Before you set your hand to that work, had not you better come down from your cross?"

Not only the rude populace, but the reverend members of the Sanhedrin, priests and scribes and Pharisees, joined in the mockery. Standing a group by themselves, they feasted upon His agony; sardonically they contrasted His going about and helping others with His present helpless plight. Their voices rose louder as they strove to drown the silent testimony of the superscription; they challenged Him to make good His title or confess Himself an impostor. His silence goaded them to ever wilder utterances; they offered to believe in Him if He would come down from the cross to which their unbelief had fastened Him.

Higher and higher rose the waves of execration, until even the crucified robbers added their fainter voices to the general blasphemy. They sought to escape insult by ingratiating themselves with the crowd and by diverting attention to their fellow sufferer.

In the midst of this sea of reproach, reviled by high and low, by living and dying, Jesus remained in complete silence. The taunts and gibes tore great wounds in His soul, more painful than those in His tortured flesh. But no word came from His lips. He was oppressed and He was afflicted, yet He opened not His mouth; He was brought as a lamb to the slaughter, and as a sheep before her shearers is dumb, so He opened not His mouth. He had poured out His soul in the First Word on the Cross. To that He would hold, whatever men might do.

> And all three hours His silence cried
> For mercy on the souls of men.

II

"The pain of the body is but the body of pain; the very soul of sorrow and pain is the soul's sorrow and pain." Thou, Lord Jesus, didst endure both the body and the soul of pain, the pain of the body and the sorrow of the soul. Thou wast pleased to suffer Thy holy body to be bruised and buffeted until it was no more than one huge stripe. Thy mouth was stung by the serpent kiss of Judas; Thy wrists were cut by tightly drawn cords; Thy face was beaten with palm and fist; Thy breast and back were lacerated with the scourge; Thy brow was pierced with thorns, and Thy face defiled with spitting; Thy body was crushed to earth under the heavy cross; Thy hands and feet were pierced through with sharp nails, and all Thy limbs were wrenched asunder on the tree; Thy mouth was parched with thirst, and Thy strength was dried up. Verily from the sole of Thy foot even unto Thy head there was no soundness in Thee, but wounds and bruises and festering sores.

But keener far, O good Jesus, O gracious Jesus, was the sorrow and pain of Thy pure soul. Thy heaviness of spirit, Thine agony and bloody sweat, the heedlessness of Thy slumbering disciples, the treason of Judas, the denial of Peter, and the flight of all Thy friends; the brutality of Thy captors, the injustice of Thy three judges, the falseness of the witnesses, the scorn of Pilate; the envy of the priests, the hardening of Thy people's hearts against Thee; the fourfold mocking, in the hall of Caiaphas, the court of Herod, the praetorium of the governor, and on the cross—lo! these were the scourging, the crowning with thorns, the crucifixion of Thy soul. O Man of Sorrows, acquainted with grief in all Thy limbs and members, and in every faculty of Thy mind and soul! thus have my sins marred Thee and my reproach hath broken Thy heart. I give Thee thanks for every wound, for every drop of blood, for Thy anguish of heart, and all Thine unknown sorrows. By those scornful and blasphemous words which, hanging on the Cross, Thou heardest spoken unto Thee, let me not be put to confusion. Oh, forbid that I should ever crucify Thee afresh and put Thee to an open shame. Teach me by Thy example to bear humbly and in silence all bodily pain and anguish of soul. Good Jesus, be Thy shame my glory, Thy pain my joy.

III

For the Merits of Christ's Reviling

O JESUS! VERY, GLORY OF THE ANGELS! Paradise of delights! Call to mind that heaviness and shuddering of Thine, when Thy cruel enemies, like ravening wolves, beset Thee, tearing Thy flesh with sharp nails, and assailing Thee with blows and spitting, and many another untold pain. By these pains, by all the reproachful gibes, by the cruel tortures which Thy enemies put upon Thee, save me, O Lord Jesus, I pray Thee, and set me free from the enemies I see around me; grant me under the shadow of Thy wings to come to perfect and everlasting safety. *Amen.*

For Patience Under Reproach

O LORD JESUS CHRIST, Who upon the Cross wast reviled of all them that passed by: Grant that I may not be delivered to the taunts and blasphemies of the devil, and that I may take with patience the reproaches of evil men; through Thy mercy, O my Lord. *Amen.*

For the Enemies and Revilers of the Church

O CHRIST, THE SON OF GOD, Who didst bear the revilings of unbelieving men when they carried Thee away to judgment: Hear our prayer, and show Thy power, we beseech Thee, towards the enemies of Thy Church, that they who persecute Thee daily in Thy members, being converted to the mystery of the faith, may gratefully acknowledge along with us that Thou wast delivered for the ungodly, and that the ungodly attain to righteousness by the glory of Thy Passion, Who livest and reignest with the Father and the Holy Ghost, One God, world without end. *Amen.*

IV

CALVARY

Friendless and faint, with martyred steps and slow,
Faint for the flesh, but for the spirit free,
Stung by the mob that came to see the show,
The Master toiled along to Calvary;
We gibed Him, as He went, with houndish glee,
Till His dimmed eyes for us did overflow;
We cursed His vengeless hands thrice wretchedly—
And this was nineteen hundred years ago.
But after nineteen hundred years the shame
Still clings, and we have not made good the loss
That outraged faith has entered in His name.
Ah, when shall come love's courage to be strong!
Tell me, O Lord—tell me, O Lord, how long
Are we to keep Christ writhing on the cross!

✝

GOOD JESUS, MOCKED AND BLASPHEMED FOR LOVE OF ME,
MAKE ME TRULY HUMBLE FOR LOVE OF THEE

The Fifth Tuesday

30. THE PENITENT ROBBER

He shall see of the travail of His soul: and shall be satisfied.

By His knowledge shall my righteous servant justify many: for He shall bear their iniquities.

Luke 23:39-43

And one of the malefactors that were hanged railed on Him, saying, Art Thou not the Christ? Save Thyself and us. But the other answered, and rebuking him said, Dost thou not even fear God, seeing thou art in the same condemnation? And we indeed justly; for we receive the due reward of our deeds: but this man hath done nothing amiss. And he said, Jesus, remember me when Thou comest in Thy kingdom. And He said unto him, Verily I say unto thee, To-day shalt thou be with me in Paradise.

I

Both robbers joined at first in the mockery of Jesus. But soon the voice of one of them grew fainter, and then fell silent altogether. Presently he called across to his fellow robber and rebuked him for his blasphemy. Finally he threw in his lot with Jesus and cast himself on His mercy.

The conversation between Jesus and the penitent robber calls to mind a conversation in a prison in Egypt, centuries before, between Joseph and Pharaoh's chief butler. According to Joseph's interpretation of his dream the butler was presently to be reinstated in office. "But think on me," the Hebrew captive added, "when it shall be well with thee, and show kindness, I pray thee, with me, and make mention of me to Pharaoh and bring me out of this place." Here on Calvary was One also about to be raised to high honor, who was besought by His companion in misery to think on him when it should be well with Him. Here, too, was a third, like the chief baker, in the same condemnation, for whom there was no hope.

Whether or not this parallel was in the mind of the robber, it may well have been in Jesus' mind. For in contrast to the sad sequel in Joseph's story—"yet did not the chief butler remember Joseph, but forgat him" —Jesus replied to His suppliant, "Verily I say unto thee, To-day shalt thou be with me in Paradise." There was to be no long season of forgetfulness; his plea would be granted that very day. He was to be with Jesus, where He was; and where Jesus is, there blossoms Paradise. "With me!"—it meant joy unspeakable for the dying robber. But no less for Jesus. Now He began to see of the travail of His soul and to be satisfied. The Second Word of the Cross expresses the meaning of the Passion on its manward side. The Father forgives, and the sinner repents. Woven into the Passion of the Saviour is the penitence of the saved. Jesus was despised and rejected by all, yet God gave Him this precious soul for His own. The bloody Tree began to bud and put forth its earliest flower. And in His agony, amid

the gibes of the multitude, He heard the first faint
note of the song of the ten thousand times ten thousand,
—"Worthy is the Lamb that was slain to receive power,
and riches, and wisdom, and strength, and honor, and
glory, and blessing."

As for the robber, how wistfully he waited for the
opening of the gate to Paradise; how lonely he felt
when Jesus bowed the head and yielded up the ghost;
how glad he was when the soldiers came and broke
his legs, that he might run the more swiftly to the
side of his King!

II

"Say, bold but blessèd Thief,
That in a trice
Slipped into Paradise,
And in plain day
Stol'st Heaven away,
What trick couldst thou invent
To compass thy intent?
What arms?
What charms?"
"Love and belief."

O Thou at whose right hand there are pleasures for
evermore! I behold in this Thief a miracle of penitence
and faith. How painfully he turns upon his cross to
watch every movement of Thine! How he strains his
ears and listens for every word that falls from Thy lips!
He notes Thy noble and patient bearing, he marvels
to see the arrows of ridicule and reproach glance from
Thee, as if Thou wert clad in magic armor. Instead
of complaints he hears from Thee only a prayer for

mercy on Thy foes. Suddenly it flashes upon him that the superscription on Thy Cross is true, that this is indeed a king! He is convinced that Thou hast done nothing amiss. Then, like a black tide, his own vileness rolls over him, and he confesses that he is receiving the just reward of his misspent life. He rebukes his fellow and yearns to share with him his penitence, as he had shared his sin. Thus he makes the leap of faith. If this Man can pray for pardon upon His murderers, surely He will not cast me off! "Jesus," he cries, reading the name from the title above Thy head, "Jesus, remember me, when Thou comest in Thy Kingdom." A modest plea—he asks not for a place in the kingdom, at Thy right hand or Thy left, but merely for a corner in the memory of the King.

> "Say, bold but blessèd Thief,
> How couldst thou read
> A crown upon that Head?
> What text, what gloss—
> A kingdom and a cross?
> How couldst thou come to spy
> God in a man to die?
> What light?
> What sight?"
> "The sight of grief."

O admirable penitence! O marvelous faith! I know not if greater faith was ever found on earth. O mighty power of Thy Cross, good Jesus! in a moment to blot out a whole life's arrears, and make a vile thief worthy to walk with Thee in Paradise! With what joy Thou didst utter this Thy Second Word on the Cross! So

Thou comest home, thorn-bruised and foot-weary and all forspent, yet with Thy lost sheep upon Thy shoulder. Good Shepherd, even so bring me home, too. Lord, remember me! Let Thy Cross and precious Blood work in me such penitence, such faith. O Christ, who art my Paradise, let me be in Thee, and walk in Thee, now while it is called To-day, and in that day when Thou shalt come in Thy kingdom.

III

The Second Word

We adore Thee, O Christ, and we bless Thee,
Because by Thy Cross and precious Blood
Thou hast redeemed the world.

O MOST BELOVED LORD JESUS CHRIST, Who for love of me didst suffer agonies on the Cross, and Who with such readiness and lovingkindness didst reward the faith of the Penitent Thief, when in the midst of Thy humiliation he acknowledged Thee to be the Son of God; O Thou Who hadst mercy on him, and didst promise him to be with Thee in Paradise: Have mercy on all Christians at their death, and on me in my last agony. Through the merits of Thy most precious Blood give me such firm and unwavering faith in Thee that my faith may not be shaken by any suggestion of the devil, and that I may attain to dwell with Thee in Paradise. *Amen.*

OUR FATHER.

GLORY BE TO THE FATHER.

211

Have mercy on us, O Lord,
Have mercy on us.

O my God, I believe in Thee, I hope in Thee, I love
Thee, and I grieve that I have so often wounded Thee
by my sins.

For a Place at Christ's Right Hand

LORD JESUS CHRIST, Son of the living God, Who
didst descend from heaven to earth, out of the bosom
of the Father, and didst sustain five wounds upon the
wood of the Cross, and shed Thy precious Blood for
the remission of our sins: We humbly beseech Thee
that at the day of judgment we may be set at Thy right
hand, and be thought worthy to hear those sweetest
words, "Come, ye blessed, into the Kingdom of my
Father"; Who with the same Father and the Holy
Ghost livest and reignest, One God, world without
end. *Amen.*

For Hardened Sinners

WE PRAY TO THEE, O LORD, for all who live wil-
fully in sin, and harden their hearts against Thee (especially . . .). Excite them, good Lord, to contrition;
melt their impenitent hearts; open their eyes that they
may behold the peril of their souls; draw them out of
the mire where they are sinking; convert them, and
they shall live. Though they have desperately sinned,
yet do Thou of Thine infinite mercy forgive them.
Let not these poor souls, so blind, so dead in sins,

perish in the everlasting fires. Show now upon them Thy mercy, and waken out of their most fearful sleep those who are in such great need of repentance and forgiveness; through Jesus Christ our Lord. *Amen.*

IV

"JESUS, PITYING THE SIGHS"

Jesus, pitying the sighs
Of the thief who near Thee dies,
Promising him Paradise:
 Hear us, Holy Jesus.

May we in our guilt and shame
Still Thy love and mercy claim,
Calling humbly on Thy Name:
 Hear us, Holy Jesus.

May our hearts to Thee incline,
Looking from our cross to Thine;
Cheer our souls with hope divine:
 Hear us, Holy Jesus.

✠

LORD JESUS, REMEMBER ME FOR GOOD

The Sixth Wednesday

31. THE VIRGIN MOTHER AND THE BELOVED DISCIPLE

I have trodden the winepress alone: and of the people there was none with me.

Who is my mother or my brethren: whosoever shall do the will of God, the same is my brother, and my sister and mother.

John 19:25-27

There were standing by the cross of Jesus His mother, and His mother's sister, Mary the wife of Clopas, and Mary Magdalene. When Jesus therefore saw His mother, and the disciple standing by whom He loved, He saith unto His mother, Woman, behold thy son! Then saith He to the disciple, Behold, thy mother! And from that hour the disciple took her unto his own home.

I

After His Father's business and His brother's need Jesus' next concern was the welfare of His mother. This was always the order, from His first recorded saying onward. Thus it was in the temple—"Wist ye not that I must be about my Father's business?" Thus it was at the marriage feast in Cana—"Woman, what have I to do with thee?" Thus it was on Calvary—"He saith unto His mother, Woman, behold, thy son! Then saith He to the disciple, Behold, thy mother!" His words breathed the purest affection and filial reverence, yet they put a distance between Him and His mother. Now He was no more her son, John was to fill that place toward her; she was no longer His mother, what she had been to Him she was to be henceforth to John. Throughout His ministry the tie between them had been loosening, until now it was finally severed. That was the sword foretold by Simeon, which here pierced through her soul. Mary must lose her Son, in order to find her Saviour. Far from bearing an active part in His saving work, she was but one of the many women upon earth—albeit most highly favored among them in that she had given Him birth—who must be saved by Jesus' blood and by faith in His merit.

The Third Word on the Cross sets forth the solitariness of the Passion. "I have trodden the winepress alone, and of the people there was none with me." He was alone in His conflict, alone in His victory. No one helped Him. The disciples had forsaken Him and fled. Of the little group of friends under the cross, these two were the nearest and dearest—Mary on whose breast He had lain, and John who had lain on His breast; and He gave them to each other; He did not need them. With a stern tenderness He cast them off. He was alone; yet not alone, because the Father was with Him.

By severing the earthly tie that bound Him to His loved ones Jesus united them the more closely to Himself and to each other. From that moment John took Mary to his own home. What sacred hours were theirs, what precious memories of the Son and Friend, who was now the Saviour in heaven, and who seemed nearer to them and more real than when their eyes had looked upon Him and their hands touched Him. Daily they found themselves becoming in a new sense His mother and His brother, while they kept the will of God which He had laid upon them with His dying breath.

II

At the Cross her station keeping
Stood the mournful Mother weeping,
   Where He hung, her dying Lord;
For her soul of joy bereaved,
Bowed with anguish, deeply grieved,
   Felt the sharp and piercing sword.

Thou, good Jesus, didst take upon Thee, besides the bitter pain of the Cross, the anguish of Thy mother's breaking heart. The sword that pierced her soul went through Thy soul also. As Thou didst rejoice with her at Cana, so Thou didst weep with her on Calvary. How sore a grief it was to Thee that by Thy suffering Thou must cause her to suffer, that by giving Thyself for all Thou must withdraw Thyself from her. O good Son! O gentle and thoughtful love! Thou Who wast about to be forsaken of Thy Father, hadst no thought but for Thy mother's forsaken and lonely heart. With pity unspeakable Thou didst provide for her a place in the home of Thy dearest earthly friend, not only to spare her the sight of Thy dying agony, but to give her, as companion for the residue of her days, the disciple likest Thee in look and tone. O Mother most sorrowful and most beloved! Now let thy soul magnify the Lord, and thy spirit rejoice in God thy Saviour. Now shall all generations call thee blessed. Blessed is the womb that bare Him, and the breasts which He hath sucked; yea, rather blessed is she that heard and kept the Word of God.

I praise and adore Thee, Jesus my only Saviour, for this Thy perfect love, Thy filial tenderness, by which Thou hast hallowed for all Thy followers the Fourth Commandment. Henceforth it is not only the first commandment with promise, but it is sealed, it is sanctified, with Thy dying breath and written in Thy blood. By this Thy loving care for Mary and for John Thou didst consecrate all human relationships and bind them to Thy Cross for ever. My thoughts dwell upon that blessed home in Jerusalem, and upon its holy inmates held together by ties closer than those of flesh and blood. How Mary must have loved John, remembering that he stood in Jesus' place; how John must have striven to be to her what her divine Son had been! It was as if Thou, their Lord in heaven, hadst come back and wert living with them under the same roof. Thrice blessed home! Hither let all parents and children turn their eyes; let parents learn of Mary to be pure and lowly and believing; and children learn of Jesus and His favored disciple to care tenderly for their parents, especially in old age and to gray hairs, and in time of trouble and need. O Wonder-worker of Cana and of Calvary! Thy first miracle and Thy last join hands and hallow for all time the homes of Thy saints, increasing their joy and consecrating their grief

—turning the water into wine, keeping the good wine till last.

III

The Third Word

We adore Thee, O Christ, and we bless Thee,
Because by Thy Cross and precious Blood Thou hast redeemed the world.

O MOST BELOVED LORD JESUS CHRIST, Who for love of me didst suffer agonies on the Cross, and forgetful of Thine own sufferings in Thy care for Thy blessed Mother didst commend her to the love of Thy beloved disciple, and thus leave us such an example of Thy Love: Have mercy on all Christians at their death, and on me in my last agony. Preserve ever in my heart a firm hope in the infinite merits of Thy most precious Blood, that I may be a partaker of Thy Love, and through Thee may be saved from the eternal misery which my sins have deserved.

OUR FATHER.

GLORY BE TO THE FATHER.

Have mercy on us, O Lord.
Have mercy on us.

O my God, I believe in Thee, I hope in Thee, I love Thee, and I grieve that I have so often wounded Thee by my sins.

For Grace to Keep the Fourth Commandment

O LORD OUR GOD, Who commandest us to honor our fathers and our mothers: Grant us so to fear and love Thee, that we may not despise nor displease our parents and superiors, but honor, serve, obey, and love them dearly; through Jesus Christ, Mary's good Son, Who is over all, God blessed for ever. *Amen.*

For the Spirit of John the Beloved

O LORD JESUS CHRIST, Who from the Tree didst behold Thy Mother and the Disciple whom Thou lovedst: Look upon me with the eyes of Thy love, and grant that I may not flee from Thy Cross, but willingly discharge whatever duty Thou layest upon me. *Amen.*

IV
"JESUS, LOVING TO THE END"

Jesus, loving to the end
Her whose heart Thy sorrows rend,
And Thy dearest human friend:
 Hear us, Holy Jesus.

May we in Thy sorrows share,
For Thy sake all peril dare,
And enjoy Thy tender care:
 Hear us, Holy Jesus.

May we all Thy loved ones be,
All one holy family,
Loving for the love of Thee:
 Hear us, Holy Jesus.

✠

JESUS, EVER MAKE ME MORE LIKE THEE

The Sixth Thursday

32. FORSAKEN

Surely, He hath borne our griefs, and carried our sorrows: He was wounded for our transgressions, He was bruised for our iniquities.

All we like sheep have gone astray: and the Lord hath laid on Him the iniquity of us all.

Matthew 27:45-46

(Mark 15:33-34)

Now from the sixth hour there was darkness over all the land, until the ninth hour. And about the ninth hour Jesus cried with a loud voice, saying, Eli, Eli, Lama Sabachthani? That is, My God, my God, why hast Thou forsaken me?

I

Darkness, the outward shadow and symbol of the gloom in Jesus' soul, covered the scene for three hours. With the darkness a deep silence fell upon Calvary, silence on the part of the Sufferer hidden from sight and on the part of the multitude under the cross; even the sounds of mockery and derision were hushed. Then, as though the darkness had found a voice, came the piercing cry, "My God, my God, why hast Thou forsaken me?"

The Fourth Word on the Cross expresses the perfect identification of Jesus with sinful mankind. He took

His place not outside and apart from the race, but at its very centre, so that the burden of the whole world's guilt was gathered up and rolled upon Him. So completely did He stand on the side of man that God seemed far away. The sin of the race rose like a wall about Him and hid the Father's face. He was one with Judas, and Caiaphas, and Pilate, and Herod, and the rude soldiers, and the mocking multitude, and the thief on the left hand; were they not all His brethren, flesh of His flesh and bone of His bone? He was the Son of Man engulfed in the universal sinfulness, and from His lips came the cry of a lost and condemned humanity, "My God, my God, why hast Thou forsaken me?"

The words are a quotation from the Old Testament prayer book. When the agony was greatest He was least individual; old human phrases rose of themselves to His lips. As the sin He was bearing was not His own, but man's sin, so the words in which He uttered His grief were not His own, but man's words. He poured out His soul in the most doleful verse of the Psalter, hallowed by the tears and groans of thousands of sufferers crying out for the living God. He was one not only with sinful, but with struggling and striving humanity. He was one with Peter weeping bitterly, with Mary and John walking sadly homeward, with the penitent thief dreaming on his cross of Paradise, with the centurion waiting to make his good confession. On His lips the words became the cry of a world perishing in guilt, yet clinging to God by the hand of Him

who alone could truly say, "My God," because He was
the Son of God. As He uttered them the darkness lifted
and the light returned.

II

Deserted! God could separate from His own essence rather;
And Adam's sins have swept between the righteous Son and
    Father;
Yea, once Immanuel's orphaned cry His universe hath
    shaken—
It went up single, echoless, "My God, I am forsaken!"
It went up from the Holy lips, amid His lost creation,
That of the lost, no son should use those words of desolation.

O Jesus, wrapped in darkness and uttering that great
and piteous cry out of the depths! Now the waters are
come in unto Thy soul, the bitter waters are gone over
Thy head. Thou hangest on the Tree, abandoned by
man and by God. Because Thou heldest fast to Thy
loving Father and wouldst not let Him go, therefore
men forsook Thee and turned against Thee. Because
Thy delights were to be with the children of men, and
despite their guilt and sin Thou wouldst not let them
go, therefore Thy holy Father forsook Thee and hid
His face from Thee. Left alone by man, Thou foundest
refuge with God, clinging to Him with the hand of
faith; forsaken of God, Thou heldest fast to man, en-
folding him with Thine arms of love. Deprived of all
his dear possessions, and like unto Job in this respect,
Thou wouldst not curse God and die, but like unto
Moses, Thou wast pleased to be anathema for Thy
brethren and kinsmen according to the flesh. Thus,
abandoned by man and by God, Thou broughtest both

together and by Thy loneliness didst unite them in holy fellowship. O Love most merciful and most mighty! O Faithfulness unto death! Though man forsook Thee, yet didst not Thou forsake him, but like Ruth Thou saidst, "Intreat me not to leave thee, or to return from following after thee: for whither thou goest, I will go; and where thou lodgest, I will lodge; thy people shall be my people, and thy God my God: where thou diest, will I die, and there will I be buried." Though God forsook Thee, yet didst not Thou forsake Him; but when Thou couldst no longer behold the face of the Father, Thou didst clasp the feet of God in the darkness. Like unto Jacob Thou didst hold Him fast until the day broke and the shadows fled away; and when He said, "Let me go," Thou saidst unto Him, "I will not let Thee go, except Thou bless me."

Now God be praised, who is with us alway and will never forsake us. And blessed be Thy holy Name, O Immanuel, for ever and ever. Nothing shall henceforth be able to separate us from the love of God, which is in Christ Jesus our Lord. If Zion say, "The Lord hath forsaken me, and my Lord hath forgotten me," He saith unto her, "Can a woman forget her sucking child, that she should not have compassion on the son of her womb? Yea, they may forget, yet will I not forget thee." As for me, if I cannot see Thee present, I will mourn Thee absent; for this also is a proof of love. Yea, though I walk through the valley of the shadow of death, I will fear no evil: for Thou art with me: Thy rod and Thy staff, which together form the holy Cross, they comfort me.

223

III

The Fourth Word

We adore Thee, O Christ, and we bless Thee,
Because by Thy Cross and precious Blood Thou hast
redeemed the world.

O JESUS! ROYAL IN THY MIGHT, and thrilling in Thy presence in the soul! Call to mind that sore distress and agony of Thine, when forlorn and desolate in the bitterness of death, and assailed by the Jews, Thou criedst with a loud voice to Thy Father, "My God, my God, why hast Thou forsaken me?" By this Thy sore distress, I beseech Thee, forsake us not in our distresses, O Lord our God. *Amen.*

OUR FATHER.

GLORY BE TO THE FATHER.

Have mercy on us, O Lord.
Have mercy on us.

O my God, I believe in Thee, I hope in Thee, I love Thee, and I grieve that I have so often wounded Thee by my sins.

For Grace to Cleave to Christ

O LORD JESUS, Who for my sins wast pleased to be forsaken of God: Grant me grace never to forsake Thee, but to cleave to Thee with unfailing love. In my darkness and distress support me with Thy very present help, and at my last hour take me to be with the Father and with Thee; through Thy mercy and for Thy merit, O my Lord. *Amen.*

For the Lonely

Lord Jesus, I beseech Thee by the loneliness of Thy suffering on the Cross, be nigh unto all of them that are desolate in pain or sorrow to-day; and let the magic of Thy Presence transform their loneliness into consolation and holy fellowship with Thee, Lord Jesus, Thou pitiful Saviour. *Amen.*

IV

THE CRUCIFIXION

Oh, man's capacity
For spiritual sorrow, corporal pain!
Who has explored the deepmost of that sea.
With heavy links of a far-fathoming chain?

That melancholy lead,
Let down in guilty and in innocent hold,
Yea, into childish hands delivered,
Leaves the sequestered floor unreached, untold.

One only has explored
The deepmost; but He did not die of it.
Not yet, not yet He died. Man's human Lord
Touched the extreme; it is not infinite.

But over the abyss
Of God's capacity for woe He strayed
One hesitating hour; what gulf was this?
Forsaken He went down, and was afraid.

✠

GOOD JESUS, TEACH ME BY THY LONELINESS
TO BE ALONE WITH THEE

The Sixth Friday

33. "I THIRST"

My strength is dried up like a potsherd; and my tongue cleaveth to my jaws: and Thou hast brought me into the dust of death.

He shall drink of the brook in the way: therefore shall He lift up the head.

John 19:28-29

(Matt. 27:48; Mark 15:36)

After this Jesus, knowing that all things are now finished, that the scripture might be accomplished, saith, I thirst. There was set there a vessel full of vinegar: so they put a sponge full of the vinegar upon hyssop, and brought it to His mouth.

I

The terrible hours on the cross had consumed Jesus' strength. He felt His life ebbing, and knew that His last hour was come. Everything for which He had lived and labored and suffered was finished and fulfilled. There was nothing more to do or bear; all that remained was to bow the head and die. But this final act of His life, no less than all His other acts, was to accomplish the Scriptures, the written will and word of God. It was foretold of Him that He should pour out His soul in death, that He was to make His soul an offering for sin. He Himself had always regarded His death as a part of His active ministry, and had said that

226

no man was to take His life from Him, but that He would lay it down of Himself. "I have power to lay it down and to take it again. This commandment have I received from my Father."

In order, therefore, to be able to lay down His life of Himself, He cried, "I thirst!" Death was not to steal upon Him unawares and take Him helpless in body and clouded in mind. There was to be no mere passive sinking into slumber; nowhere in Scripture is His dying called a falling asleep. He would go forth to meet the last enemy as He had met His captors in the garden, saying, "I am He." His death was to be His own deed, His conscious and deliberate act. The Fifth Word on the Cross proclaims what the older theologians were fond of calling the "active obedience" of Christ, which alone gave to His Passion its value and saving worth and made it precious in the sight of the Lord. For the same reason that He refused the drugged wine before crucifixion He now craved a stimulating potion, in order with clear mind, actively and voluntarily, to give His life a ransom for many. It was no selfish boon He desired, no refreshment of His languid spirit, nor least easing of any bodily pang. It was altogether for us, that He might love His own unto the end and think on us with His last thought; that He might gather up His remaining strength in order to spend it in the triumphant cry, "It is finished," and compel death to bear His spirit home to the Father's hands.

In contrast with the mockery that met the Fourth Word, the cry "I thirst" was followed by the last kindness shown our Lord upon earth. Whoever it was that held to His lips the sponge drenched with vinegar, may he be among them who shall hear at the last day those most gracious words, "Come, ye blessed of my Father: I was thirsty and ye gave me drink."

II

My heart is resting, O my God—
I will give thanks and sing;
My heart is at the secret source
Of every precious thing.
Now the frail vessel Thou hast made
No hand but Thine shall fill—
For the waters of the Earth have failed,
And I am thirsty still.

Sweet Jesus, Fount of living waters, Thou who hadst rest for the weary and heavy laden; who didst say, "If any man thirst, let him come unto me and drink"; and didst promise that whosoever cometh to Thee shall never hunger, and whosoever believeth on Thee shall never thirst! Weary and heavy laden with the burden of my sin Thou hangest on the Tree. Thy strength is dried up like a potsherd, Thy tongue cleaveth to Thy jaws, and Thou art brought into the dust of death. That I might not be tormented in hell, Thou criest, "I thirst!" pleading for a drop of water to cool Thy tongue. Thus Thou makest atonement for all our sins of the tongue, from the disobedience of our first parents to the lusting of their children for the fleshpots of the world. O Lord strong and mighty, O Lord mighty in battle! Thou pantest and art athirst by reason of Thy sore conflict with sin and death, treading them in Thine anger and trampling them in Thy fury, Thou Stronger One who comest upon the strong man armed, and takest from him all his armor wherein he trusted, and dividest the spoils. Even so Samson, after slaying the Philistines, was sore athirst and called upon the Lord, who gave him drink, so that his spirit came again and he revived.

Lover of men, Thy heart is wounded for love of me; Thy bodily thirst is but an image of Thy thirst for souls. Even so Thou saidst to the woman of Samaria, "Give me to drink," filled with longing for her salvation rather than for water that she could draw with her pitcher from the well. Therefore, when Thy disciples returned and prayed Thee, "Master, eat," Thou saidst, "I have meat to eat that ye know not of." Still dost Thou call, "My son, my daughter, give me thine heart." Take me, my Saviour, here am I; lo, I hold up my heart as a cup to Thy lips, and give Thee to drink. Oh, may Thy thirst upon the Cross kindle in me a thirst for Thee, the Fountain of life. Like as the hart panteth after the water brooks, so let my soul pant for Thee, O God. Give me that living water, which shall be in me a well springing up into everlasting life. Grant me also Thy burning thirst for souls, a hearty desire for the salvation of the world for which Thou didst pour out Thy blood. Bring all Thy people at last where they shall hunger no more, neither thirst any more, neither shall the sun light on them nor any heat; for Thou, the Lamb that art in the midst of the throne, shalt feed them, and shalt lead them to living fountains of waters.

III

The Fifth Word

We adore Thee, O Christ, and we bless Thee,
Because by Thy Cross and precious Blood Thou hast
redeemed the world.

O MOST BELOVED LORD JESUS CHRIST, Who for love
of me didst suffer agonies on the Cross, and Who, to
all Thy shame and all Thy sufferings, wouldest if needful have added yet more, so that all men might be
saved, since all the torments of Thy Passion did not
allay the thirst of Thy tender heart: Have pity on all
Christians at their death, and on me in my last agony.
Through the merits of Thy most precious Blood en-
kindle in my heart such a fire of Thy love, that I may
thirst for Thy glory here, and with earnest longings
desire to be united to Thee hereafter throughout the
ages of eternity. *Amen.*

OUR FATHER.

GLORY BE TO THE FATHER.

Have mercy on us, O Lord.
Have mercy on us.

O my God, I believe in Thee, I hope in Thee, I love
Thee, and I grieve that I have so often wounded Thee
by my sins.

Against the Thirst of Fleshly Lust

O JESUS! Unfailing Spring of love, Who from
the lowest depth thereof saidst upon the Cross, "I
thirst," even for man's salvation: Kindle the desires

of our hearts, I pray Thee, for every good work; allay and staunch in us wholly the thirst of every fleshly lust, and all the feverishness of this world's pleasures. *Amen.*

For the Panting of the Soul After Christ

O LORD JESUS CHRIST, let the thirst Thou didst endure upon the Tree quench the thirst of my soul, and preserve me from everlasting torment. Grant that Thy perfect sacrifice upon the altar of Calvary may be the comfort and refreshment of my soul. Make me evermore to thirst for Thee, the Fountain of life, so that in my last hour I may confidently commend my spirit into Thy hands. *Amen.*

IV

"JESUS, IN THY THIRST AND PAIN"

Jesus, in Thy thirst and pain,
While Thy wounds Thy life-blood drain,
Thirsting more our love to gain:
    Hear us, Holy Jesus.

Thirst for us in mercy still;
All Thy holy work fulfil;
Satisfy Thy loving will:
    Hear us, Holy Jesus.

My we thirst Thy love to know;
Lead us in our sin and woe
Where the healing waters flow:
    Hear us, Holy Jesus.

✠

TAKE ME, O JESUS, AND MAKE ME WHOLLY THINE

The Sixth Saturday

34. "CONSUMMATUM EST"

*And God saw every thing that He had made: and,
behold, it was very good.*

*I have glorified Thee on the earth: I have finished
the work which Thou gavest me to do.*

John 19:30

When Jesus therefore had received the vinegar, He
said, It is finished.

I

The Sixth Word on the Cross proclaims the finality of
the Passion. Whatever else was finished—the holy life,
the dreadful suffering, human taunts, and Satan's spite
—one achievement stood out above all else in Jesus'
mind, namely, the fulfillment of the Father's will to
salvation, to which He had dedicated His life. That
was the goal of all His acts, of all His sufferings, and
now it was attained. His lifework was complete. With
what care He had prepared for that work, and how
faithfully He had pursued it! In the carpenter's shop,
those many hidden years, He had made His body
strong and His soul ready, by work and prayer, for
the task before Him. At His Baptism He solemnly
consecrated Himself to its performance. In His Temptation He chose the motives by which He would be gov-

erned and the means He would employ. Throughout His public ministry He carried forward that task, never swerving for friend or foe. "I must work the works of Him that sent me, while it is day: the night cometh, when no man can work." By teaching and living, by healing and loving; through many a weary day, when He could not so much as find time to eat, and many a night spent in communion with His heavenly Father; meekly bearing misunderstanding and disappointment, malice and insult; guided at every step by the Father's will and His own love for souls—thus He built the house of life for His brethren, slowly adding stone to stone, until after the agony in the garden, the trials before Caiaphas, Pilate, and Herod, and the hours of torture on Calvary, just before the night came, He was able, high upon the ladder of the cross, to set in place the topmost stone, and the whole structure stood before Him complete and beautiful and enduring. *Consummatum est,* it is consummated, it is finished, eternal redemption is obtained!

It was a cry of trembling joy—the joy of the workman before his finished task, the joy of the artist putting the last touch to his masterpiece, the joy of the conqueror when the trumpets of victory blow. Nay, it was the counterpart of the joy of the Creator, when in the morning of the world He saw everything that He had made, and behold, it was very good. Now everything was once more very good, and with triumphant contentment the Redeemer could enter into His sabbath rest in the tomb.

II

Nothing in my hand I bring:
Simply to Thy Cross I cling.

———

This have I done for thee:
What wilt thou do for Me?

It is finished: nothing remains for me to do. Other
foundation can no man lay than that is laid; other
name there is none under heaven given among men,
whereby we must be saved. O High Priest of good
things to come, by Thine own Blood Thou didst enter
in once into the Holy Place, having obtained eternal
redemption for us. Thou art the one and only Mediator
between God and man. Not by works of righteousness
that we have done, but according to His mercy God
saved us. Hark, the call to the Marriage Feast—"Behold, I have prepared my dinner: my oxen and my
fatlings are killed, and all things are ready: come unto
the marriage!" O word of plenteous redemption! If
the law condemn me, I will say, "It is finished: Christ
is the end of the law to every one that believeth." If
Satan accuse me, I will say, "It is finished: I am more
than conqueror through Him that loved me." If my
sins oppress me, I will say, "It is finished: there is now
no condemnation to them that are in Christ Jesus."
When death draws nigh, I will say, "It is finished:
Jesus Christ hath abolished death, and brought life and
immortality to light." When I rise from the grave and
stand before the dreadful Judgment-seat, I will say,
"It is finished:—

Jesus, Thy Blood and Righteousness
My beauty are, my glorious dress."

It is finished: now my work begins. On the foundation that Thou hast laid, O all-sufficient Saviour, I would build in faith and gratitude and love and prayer. Hast not Thou said, "He that believeth on me, the works that I do shall he do also; and greater works than these shall he do; because I go unto my Father, and whatsoever ye shall ask in my name, that will I do"? Thou hast given Thyself for us, that Thou mightest redeem us from all iniquity, and purify unto Thyself a peculiar people, zealous of good works. Alas! how incomplete are our works compared to Thine. Of the best of us it must be said, "A little space was allowed him to show at least a heroic purpose, and to attest a high design: then, with all things unfinished before him and behind, he fell asleep after many troubles and triumphs." Yet, O Lord, if we set about our duties, looking unto Thee, and uniting our feeble efforts to Thy finished work, Thou wilt grant us grace to say at the last, "I have fought a good fight, I have finished my course, I have kept the faith." Nay, when we are most conscious of failure and defeat, Thou canst help us to accomplish most. For Thy grace is sufficient for us, and Thy strength is made perfect in our weakness. Thou, O Lord, art our strength and our shield; therefore, when we are weak, then are we strong. Help us to be steadfast, unmovable, always abounding in the work of the Lord, forasmuch as we know that our labor is not in vain in the Lord.

III

The Sixth Word

We adore Thee, O Christ, and we bless Thee,
Because by Thy Cross and precious Blood Thou hast
redeemed the world.

O MOST BELOVED LORD JESUS CHRIST, Who for love
of me didst suffer agonies on the Cross, and from that
throne of truth didst announce the completion of the
work of our redemption, through which from being
children of wrath we have become children of God
and heirs of eternal life: Have pity upon all Christians
at their death, and on me in my last agony. Through
the merits of Thy most precious Blood detach me
entirely from love of the world, and from love of self,
and from all creatures, and enable me to offer to Thee
the sacrifice of my life, and to seek from Thee the
pardon of all my sins. *Amen.*

OUR FATHER.

GLORY BE TO THE FATHER.

Have mercy on us, O Lord.
Have mercy on us.

O my God, I believe in Thee, I hope in Thee, I love
Thee, and I grieve that I have so often wounded Thee
by my sins.

For the Finishing of My Course

O JESUS, Author of eternal redemption, call to
mind that hour upon the Cross, when Thy heartstrings
brake, and all Thy strength gave way, and bowing

Thy head Thou saidst, "It is finished." By this Thine
anguish and Thy joy grant me so to follow in Thy
footsteps that at my last hour I may say, "I have fought
a good fight, I have finished my course, I have kept the
faith," and may lay me down in peace and sleep, and
awake after Thy likeness. *Amen.*

For Safe Lodging and Holy Rest

O LORD, support us all the day long of this troub-
lous life, until the shades lengthen, and the evening
come, and the busy world is hushed, the fever of life
is over, and our work done. Then, Lord, in Thy mercy,
grant us safe lodging, a holy rest, and peace at the
last; through Jesus Christ our Lord. *Amen.*

IV

"JESUS, ALL OUR RANSOM PAID"

Jesus, all our ransom paid,
All Thy Father's will obeyed;
By Thy sufferings perfect made:
　　Hear us, Holy Jesus.

Save us in our soul's distress;
Be our help to cheer and bless,
While we grow in holiness:
　　Hear us, Holy Jesus.

Brighten all our heavenward way
With an ever holier ray,
Till we pass to perfect day:
　　Hear us, Holy Jesus.

✠

JESUS, BE THOU TO ME ALPHA AND OMEGA

Monday in Holy Week

Thou wilt not leave my soul in hell: neither wilt Thou suffer Thy Holy One to see corruption.

The souls of the righteous are in the hands of God: and there shall no torment touch them.

Luke 23:46

(Matt. 27:50; Mark 15:37; John 19:30)

And Jesus, crying with a loud voice, said, Father, into Thy hands I commend my spirit: and having said this, He gave up the ghost.

I

Jesus' last word was a word of faith. He died with a passage of Holy Scripture upon His lips, an old psalm verse with His own authentic "Father" prefixed. His last word was in perfect accord with His first; the Father whom He found as a child in the temple He had never lost. Nothing stands out more clearly in His life and in His sufferings than His unbroken trust in the Father. Though for three black hours on the cross the sin of the world hid the Father's face, now the darkness had lifted, the sin was taken away, and He saw before Him nothing but the Father with hands outstretched. Into those hands He committed His spirit. There was no fear in Him; confidently,

238

speaking with a loud voice, He went to the Father—the Captain and Perfecter of our faith.

It was a word of hope. He was persuaded that the Father was able to keep that which He committed unto Him against that day. In His words there breathed the spirit of another stanza from the Psalter, applied afterwards by Peter to the Resurrection—"Thou wilt not leave my soul in Sheol; neither wilt Thou suffer Thy Holy One to see corruption. Thou wilt show me the path of life: in Thy presence is fulness of joy; at Thy right hand there are pleasures for evermore." The Last Word on the Cross sets forth, above all, the intimate relation between the Passion and the Resurrection. They are the two halves of an indivisible whole. Never did Jesus think of His suffering and death apart from His resurrection; always, at the close of every prediction of His Passion, He added, "and the third day He shall rise again." At the conclusion of His active ministry He had received from God the Father honor and glory, when the Voice called out of the bright cloud, "This is my beloved Son, in whom I am well pleased." Now, at the close of His Passion, He was confident that He would be declared to be the Son of God with power, by the resurrection from the dead.

It was a word of love. With His last thought He remembered His own that were in the world, and left them this precious heritage, a word of spirit and of life, which if a man keep he shall never see death, a word by which to live and with which to die. The death of Jesus is not only a ransom for all, but a pattern for His followers. Ere long He was to hear, standing at the right hand of God, His dying prayer addressed to Him by the leader of the martyr host— "Lord Jesus, receive my spirit."

II

Never weather-beaten sail more willing bent to shore,
Never tired pilgrim's limbs affected slumber more,
Than my weary spirit now longs to fly out of my troubled breast:
O come quickly, sweetest Lord, and take my soul to rest!

Good Jesus, laying down Thy life for Thine own! It is appointed unto men once to die, and we know not the day nor the hour. At death my soul is required of me; whether I will or no, my spirit must needs depart out of the house of the body and fare forth as a traveler to eternity. But Thou didst choose the time of Thy departure, and with great willingness didst pour out Thy soul in death, and with a loud and joyful cry yield up the ghost. Even so Aaron the high priest went up most willingly into Mount Hor, and suffered himself to be stripped of his garments, and died there in the top of the mount, as the Lord commanded. O great High Priest, holy, harmless, undefiled, made separate from sinners! Thou wast not under penalty of death; the prince of this world had nothing in Thee. For whom then didst Thou die if not for me? Verily, Thou didst taste death for every man. Thou Who art the Plagues of death and Destruction of the grave, Thou didst bind our souls in the bundle of life with

Thine own, and didst commend them into Thy Father's hands, from which no man is able to pluck them. O Prince of life, as Thy death is my life, even so let Thy dying word be to me a word of life. I would hide it in my heart, so that living or dying I may not sin against Thee. I would learn from it the art of dying well, which is none other than the art of living well. I would learn to die daily, to sin and self and every creature; to live soberly, righteously, and godly in this present world; to have my loins always girded and my lamp burning, like unto a servant that waiteth for his Lord.

Blessed be God my Creator! Blessed be God my Saviour! Blessed be God my Comforter! Into Thy hands I commend, this day and every day, my poor soul, my weak body, my frail life, my senses, reason, understanding and imagination, all that I do and leave undone, my coming in and my going out, my moving about and my standing still, my downsitting and mine uprising, my will and desires, my plans and purposes, my faith and confession, all that I am and all that I can do, the end of my life, the day and hour of my departure, my death and my resurrection. I commend my soul into the omnipotent hands that gave it, into the fatherly hands in which no torment shall touch it, into the faithful hands that are able to keep it against that day. For me to live is Christ, and to die is gain. O Thou in whose death God hath graven me upon the palms of His hands, Lord Jesus, receive my spirit.

III

The Seventh Word

We adore Thee, O Christ, and we bless Thee,
Because by Thy Cross and precious Blood Thou hast redeemed the world.

O MOST BELOVED JESUS CHRIST, Who for love of me didst suffer agonies on the Cross, and Who, to complete so great a sacrifice, didst accept the will of Thy Father by resigning Thy spirit into His hands, and bowing Thy head and dying: Have mercy on all Christians at their death, and on me in my last agony. Through the merits of Thy most precious Blood give me in my last moments an entire conformity to Thy Divine will, so that I may be ready to live or die, as it shall best please Thee, desiring nothing but that Thy holy will should be done in me and by me. *Amen.*

OUR FATHER.

GLORY BE TO THE FATHER.

Have mercy on us, O Lord.
Have mercy on us.

O my God, I believe in Thee, I hope in Thee, I love Thee, and I grieve that I have so often wounded Thee by my sins.

For the Blessing of Jesus' Death

O JESUS! Only-Begotten of the Father most high, Brightness and Image of His glory: Call to mind that strong yearning effort when Thou criedst to the Father, "Into Thy hands I commend my spirit"; when with body torn and heart broken, with one mighty cry

Thou gavest up the ghost. By this Thy most precious death, I pray Thee, give me strength to withstand the devil, the world, and the flesh, that being dead to sin I may live to Thee; and in the last hour of my departure hence, receive my soul returning again an exile and a stranger unto Thee. *Amen.*

"Deliver Us from Evil"

OUR FATHER IN HEAVEN, deliver us, we pray Thee, from all manner of evil, whether it touch our body or soul, our property or good name; and at last, when the hour of death shall come, grant us a blessed end, and graciously take us from this vale of sorrow to Thyself in heaven; for Thine is the kingdom, and the power, and the glory for ever and ever. *Amen.*

IV

DOMINUS ILLUMINATIO MEA

In the hour of death, after this life's whim,
When the heart beats low, and the eyes grow dim,
And pain has exhausted every limb—
　　The lover of the Lord shall trust in Him.

When the will has forgotten the lifelong aim,
And the mind can only disgrace its fame,
And a man is uncertain of his own name
　　The power of the Lord shall fill this frame.

When the last sigh is heaved, and the last tear shed,
And the coffin is waiting beside the bed,
And the widow and child forsake the dead—
　　The angel of the Lord shall lift this head.

THE MAN OF SORROWS

For even the purest delight may pall,
And power must fail, and the pride must fall,
And the love of the dearest friends grow small—
But the glory of the Lord is all in all.

✠

LORD JESUS, SHOW ME THE PATH OF LIFE

Tuesday in Holy Week

He did wonders in His life: and at His death were His works marvelous.

God is a Spirit: and they that worship Him must worship Him in spirit and in truth.

Mark 15:38-39

(Matt. 27:51-54; Luke 23:45, 47-48)

And the veil of the temple was rent in two from the top to the bottom. And when the centurion, who stood by over against Him, saw that He so gave up the ghost, he said, Truly this man was the Son of God.

I

Jesus' death, no less than His birth, was accompanied by miraculous signs. Matthew gives a complete list: the rending of the temple curtain, the earthquake, the opening of the tombs of saints, the confession of the centurion. Mark mentions only the first and last, as the most important.

There was a curtain before the Holy of Holies and one before the Holy Place, and it is a question which of the two is meant. If we connect the tearing of the curtain with the earthquake, and follow Jewish and early Christian tradition, we shall decide in favor of the latter. The meaning of this sign will then lie not merely in the throwing open of Israel's inner sanctuary but in the beginning of the destruction of the temple as such, in the spirit of Jesus' saying, "The hour cometh, when ye shall neither in this mountain, nor yet at Jerusalem, worship the Father." The Jewish temple had been for centuries the appointed place of God's presence and of man's sacrifice. Now that Immanuel had come, in whom dwelleth all the fullness of the Godhead bodily, and had offered the perfect Sacrifice, the temple building became useless and began to crumble. It stood, an empty and meaningless shell, for forty years longer, and was then destroyed.

Not less significant was the confession of the centurion, which may be regarded as a counterpart to the rending of the temple veil. This hardened man of war, who had doubtless presided unmoved over many similar executions, was profoundly impressed by the manner of Jesus' passing. He had been observing Him closely and pondering His sayings. Now he gave expression to his feeling in the words, "This man was certainly a Son of God." Both feeling and expression are entirely heathen, and we must not set too high a value upon them. Luke probably comes nearest to what he really said—"Certainly this was a righteous man"; for "Son of God" could scarcely have meant much more than this in the mouth of a Roman soldier. Nevertheless, it was an honest conviction honestly expressed, a taking sides not without grave personal risk with his dead Prisoner. Without crediting the tradition that named him Longinus, made him bishop, and ascribed to him a martyr's death, we may well believe that here was the first stirring in a Gentile breast of faith in the Crucified. Slowly the congregation of believers is seen to be forming about the cross. First it was the penitent robber, now the centurion is added, and Joseph and Nicodemus are on the way. Thus the "two or three" are gathering together in the name of Him who died upon the cross, and before long He Himself will be in their midst with His abundant life.

II

Greater than Elisha, O Thou who performedst mighty wonders in Thy life, and whose works were marvelous at Thy death! Thou hast removed the veil from the heart of God, so that sinful man may draw nigh in true faith, without fear. At Thy death the temple curtain was rent in twain, and God's ancient dwelling began to pass away. Now they that worship the Father must worship Him in spirit and in truth. Not in Jerusalem was the perfect Offering made; Thou didst suffer without the gate. Henceforth God dwelleth not in darkness, behind heavy curtains, in a hidden shrine. Not in the smoke of sacrifice is He found, nor in mysterious priestly ceremonial; but in water flowing under the open sky, in bread and wine growing in the fields, in the word sounding through streets and lanes and along highways and hedges. O Only-begotten Son, Thou hast revealed the Father, in Thy holy life and by Thy precious death. Jerusalem is now everywhere. Wherever two or three are gathered together in Thy name, Thou art in the midst of them; and where Thou art, there is the Father with shining face and hands outspread. Through Thee we have boldness and access with confidence by faith.

Thou hast removed the veil from the heart of man, so that God may draw near unhindered with His saving grace. At Thy death the veil before the centurion's soul was rent in twain from the top to the bottom. The curtain of ignorance by which his foolish heart was darkened, and of sinful pride that shut him in, was torn asunder, and his soul lay open to God. With his heart he believed unto righteousness, and with his mouth he made confession unto salvation. This was the Lord's doing, and it is marvelous in our eyes. O precious fruit of Thy dying love, and earnest of the harvest to be! Thus didst Thou break down the middle wall of partition between Jew and Gentile and make both one. But behold, O Lord our Peace, the minds of Thine own people are blinded still; even to this day the veil is upon their hearts. Wilt Thou not turn them speedily to Thee, that the veil may be taken away? Remove also from my soul veil after veil, that Thou mayest come unto me with Thy Father and make Thy abode with me. Let my body be the temple of the Holy Ghost, and my mind Thy sanctuary, enlightened by Thy Word, sweetened with incense of prayer, and hallowed by the whole burnt offering of my will. Nay, do Thou pursue me with Thy truth even to the inward parts, and in the hidden part make me to know wisdom.

Father, Son and Holy Spirit, Blessed Trinity! bring us all at last to behold with open face Thy unveiled glory for ever.

III

For Boldness to Enter the Holiest

GOD, WHO DOST MOST affectionately encourage us to believe that Thou art truly our Father and that we are Thy children indeed: Grant that we may call upon Thee with all cheerfulness and confidence, even as beloved children entreat their beloved parent; through Jesus Christ Thine Only-begotten Son our Lord. *Amen.*

For Faith in Christ As God

O LORD JESUS CHRIST, Who wast declared by manifold signs accompanying Thy death to be the Son of God and King of creation: Grant that with my whole heart I may acknowledge Thee as very God of very God, and by this faith overcome the world. Stretch out Thine arms upon the Cross to embrace me and hide me in Thy sacred wounds. *Amen.*

"Draw us to Thee, Lord Jesus"

O FAITHFUL SAVIOUR, we praise Thee, Who didst even on the Cross begin to fulfill Thy words, "If I be lifted up from the earth, I will draw all men unto me." May it please Thee to draw those who are far from Thee and still harbor a sinful contempt of Thy reproach. Teach them to acknowledge Thy ignominious death as the only means whereby our death may be overcome and the guilt of our sins blotted out. Incline all our hearts to contemplate Thy meritorious

death, and grant that we may enjoy its precious fruits.
Rend the veil of our prejudices, shake our hard and
obdurate hearts, and open the grave of our sins, that
we may come forth to new life. Grant us to beat our
breasts in godly sorrow and return from our evil ways.
Thus, O blessed Jesus, may all that passed outwardly
at Thy death be accomplished within us. Have mercy
upon us, O Lamb of God, and hear us for the sake
of Thy precious Passion and Death. *Amen.*

IV

THE DEAD CHRIST

That Sacrifice!—the death of Him—
   The High and ever Holy One!
Well may the conscious Heaven grow dim,
   And blacken the beholding Sun.
The wonted light hath fled away,
Night settles in the middle day,
And earthquake from his caverned bed
Is waking with a thrill of dread.

The dead are waking underneath!
   Their prison door is rent away!
And, ghastly with the seal of death,
   They wander in the eye of day!
The temple of the Cherubim,
The House of God, is cold and dim;
A curse is on its trembling walls,
Its mighty veil asunder falls.

Well may the cavern-depths of earth
   Be shaken, and her mountains nod;
Well may the sheeted dead come forth
   To gaze upon a suffering God!

THE RENDING OF THE VEILS

Well may the temple shrine grow dim,
And shadows veil the Cherubim,
When He, the chosen one of Heaven,
A sacrifice for guilt is given!

And shall the sinful heart alone
   Behold unmoved the atoning hour,
When nature trembles on her throne,
   And Death resigns his iron power?
Oh, shall the heart,—whose sinfulness
Gave keenness to His sore distress,
And added to His tears of blood—
Refuse its trembling gratitude?

✠

LORD, SHOW US THE FATHER, AND IT SUFFICETH US

Wednesday in Holy Week

Your lamb shall be without blemish: and all the congregation of Israel shall kill it in the evening.

In the midst of the throne there stood a Lamb as it had been slain: Blessing and honor, and glory, and power be unto the Lamb for ever and ever.

John 19:31-37

The Jews therefore, because it was the Preparation, that the bodies should not remain on the cross upon the Sabbath (for the day of that Sabbath was a high day), asked of Pilate that their legs might be broken, and that they might be taken away. The soldiers therefore came, and brake the legs of the first, and of the other that was crucified with him: but when they came to Jesus and saw that He was dead already, they brake not His legs: Howbeit one of the soldiers with a spear pierced His side, and straightway there came out blood and water. And he that hath seen hath borne witness, and his witness is true: and he knoweth that he saith true, that ye also may believe. For these things came to pass, that the scripture might be fulfilled, A bone of Him shall not be broken. And again another scripture saith, They shall look on Him whom they pierced.

I

Good Friday's sun was low, and the three crosses cast long shadows upon the ground. It was contrary to Jewish law for the dead body of a criminal to remain overnight on a tree. Least of all could it be permitted on this night, for with sundown the sabbath would begin, which being the sabbath in passover week was a "high day." Hence the Jewish authorities arranged with Pilate that the three crucified should be despatched by "the breaking of the legs" and their bodies be buried. We recognize here the same moral astigmatism that we have met before in the Passion story. These men did not scruple to bring about Jesus' death, but were seized with pious horror at the thought of His body remaining on the cross to defile their holy day.

The soldiers of the governor approached to administer the *crurifragium,* that last cruel tenderness, which consisted in crushing the legs of the crucified with heavy mallets, the shock producing death. After despatching the two robbers they came to Jesus, and finding Him already dead, refrained. In this John saw the fulfillment of the old passover law, according to which not a bone of the paschal lamb might be broken. Jesus was thus declared, at the close as at the beginning of His ministry, to be the Lamb of God that taketh away the sin of the world. There was no need of the mallet, yet to make assurance doubly sure, one of the soldiers thrust his lance into Jesus' side, and John saw blood and water flow from the wound. In this he found the fulfilment of another scripture, which he regarded as foretelling that the Jews should one day look in penitent faith upon their pierced Messiah.

John solemnly attested the genuineness of his record by invoking Jesus Himself as witness. He declared that he recorded what he had seen in order that his readers might believe. He used a similar expression at the close of his Easter narrative; the signs of the Risen Lord were set down "that ye might believe that Jesus is the Christ the Son of God, and that believing ye might have life through His name." Belief in the resurrection of Jesus presupposes the certainty of His death, and this certainty John was concerned to establish, against a subtle heresy which was in the air at that time. There has been much mystical speculation as to the meaning of the flow of blood and water; yet John did not regard it as miraculous, but as the natural result of the spear-thrust; instead of considering it a sign of Jesus' persisting life, he dwelt upon it as a proof of His actual death.

II

Good Jesus, I praise Thee for Thy obedience unto death, even the death of the Cross. Now the silver cord is loosed, the golden bowl is broken. Thy soul has gone among the dead, and Thy body hangs motionless upon the Tree. Yet it is still Thy body and most precious unto Thee; for Thou wilt presently return to it, and wilt dwell in it, a glorious body, for ever. Therefore no harm, no outrage may befall it, O Lamb without blemish and without spot. The piercing of Thy side by the soldier's spear Thou didst suffer, in order that St. Thomas might thrust his hand into the wound and seeing might believe, so that we may be blessed, who not having seen yet believe that Thou wast indeed dead and art alive again, our Lord and our God.

I adore Thee, O Christ, and I bless Thee, for the fivefold shedding of Thy most holy Blood. For me Thou wast bathed in bloody sweat in the garden; for me Thou wast scourged with the cruel scourge; for me Thou wast crowned with thorns, so that Thy head and face were covered with blood; for me Thy hands and feet were pierced through; for me Thy sacred side was riven by the Roman soldier and gave forth blood and water. Lo! here is the river of God that is full of water, in which I would bathe, in which I would wash me clean from every sin. As many of us as were baptized into Thee, O Christ, were we not baptized into Thy death? By the faithful contemplation of Thy Holy Passion, grant me to fulfill the meaning of my Baptism. In the blood and water from Thy five sacred wounds I would drown and destroy, by daily sorrow and repentance, the old Adam in me together with all sins and evil lusts, and from this most cleansing flood come forth daily and rise a new man, who shall live in the presence of God in righteousness and purity for ever. Let me reckon myself to be dead indeed unto sin, but alive unto God through Jesus Christ my Lord.

To this end do Thou pierce my side with the sharp spear of Thy love, so that I may seek pardon for my wandering desires, my vain and foolish imaginations, and all the evil thoughts to which my heart gives birth. Oh, that Thou wouldest prick me in my heart, that I might ask of Thee, "What shall I do?" I am sore tempted to sloth, I grow often weary in well doing. Send down Thy holy Angel to smite me on the side, even as he smote St. Peter sleeping in prison, and said, "Arise up quickly!" I would work out my own salvation with fear and trembling, for Thou, Lord, only workest in me both to will and to do. Let me look now, in penitence and faith, on Him whom I have pierced, and when Thou shalt come to judge the quick and the dead—

> Rock of Ages, cleft for me,
> Let me hide myself in Thee!

III

For Faith in Christ Dead and Living

O CHRIST, in Whose Side upon the Cross the spear of the Roman soldier cleft so deep a wound that after Thy Resurrection Thou couldest bid St. Thomas thrust his hand therein: Grant me to believe with my whole heart that Thou art in very truth He that liveth, and was dead, and is alive for evermore, so that through this faith I may have life in Thy Name. Amen, my Lord and my God, *Amen.*

For the Gifts and Benefits of Baptism

LORD JESUS CHRIST, Who by Thy precious Blood hast redeemed me from all sins, from death, and from the power of the devil, and Who hast graciously ordained the Sacrament of Holy Baptism, which worketh forgiveness of sins, delivers from death and the devil, and confers everlasting salvation on all who believe: Grant me, redeemed by Thy Blood and baptized into Thy Death, ever more firmly to believe, that so I may be saved, as the Word and promise of God declare. *Amen.*

For the Grace of Holy Zeal

O MOST ZEALOUS HIGH PRIEST, very God and very Man, eternal praise and thanksgiving be to Thee, because Thou didst suffer Thy sacred Side to be pierced, opened, and wounded with a spear. By this most holy shedding of Thy Blood, I earnestly pray Thee for the grace of holy zeal and fervor, against all sloth and weariness in Thy service. *Amen.*

IV

"LORD OF MY HEART"

Lord of my heart, by Thy last cry,
  Let not Thy Blood on earth be spent—
Lo, at Thy feet I fainting lie,
  Mine eyes upon Thy wounds are bent,
Upon Thy streaming wounds my weary eyes
Wait like the parched earth on April skies.

Wash me, and dry these bitter tears,
  O let my heart no longer roam,
'Tis Thine by vows, and hopes, and fears,
  Long since—O call Thy wanderer home;
To that dear home, safe in Thy wounded Side,
Where only broken hearts their sin and shame may hide.

☩

LORD JESUS, HIDE ME IN THY WOUNDED SIDE

Thursday in Holy Week

And He made His grave with the wicked: and with the rich in His death.

I will both lay me down in peace, and sleep: for Thou, Lord, only makest me dwell in safety.

John 19:38-42

(Matt. 27:57-60; Mark 15:42-46; Luke 23:50-53)

And after these things Joseph of Arimathaea, being a disciple of Jesus, but secretly for fear of the Jews, asked of Pilate that he might take away the body of Jesus: and Pilate gave him leave. He came therefore, and took away His body. And there came also Nicodemus, he who at the first came to Him by night, bringing a mixture of myrrh and aloes, about a hundred pounds. So they took the body of Jesus, and bound it in linen cloths with the spices, as the custom of the Jews is to bury. Now in the place where He was crucified there was a garden; and in the garden a new tomb wherein was never man yet laid. There then because of the Jews' Preparation (for the tomb was nigh at hand) they laid Jesus.

I

The burial of Jesus brings on the scene two persons not hitherto mentioned in the Passion history, one of whom makes here his first appearance in the gospel narrative—Nicodemus, and Joseph of Arimathaea.

Joseph, a secret disciple who had kept in the background for fear of the Jews, was a rich man and a righteous, and one of those who waited for the kingdom of God. Nicodemus was well known to the readers of John's gospel as the distinguished Pharisee who had come to Jesus by night. Both were members of the Sanhedrin, and were opposed to the action of that body against Jesus; on one occasion Nicodemus had protested openly against condemning Him without a hearing. They were probably not present at the meeting in which He was sentenced to death, for Mark says that the vote was unanimous. But now they came forward and openly allied themselves with the cause of their dead Friend. There is something pathetic in this late blossoming of their faith, and yet their appearance at this hour and under such unfavorable conditions must be included among the miraculous signs attending Jesus' death.

Joseph, who was first on the scene, obtained the governor's permission to remove the body of Jesus. Under his direction it was lowered from the cross and made ready for burial. At this point Nicodemus arrived with a plentiful supply of spices. The clean linen cloth, which Joseph had purchased probably on the way back from the governor's palace, was torn into narrow strips, which were sprinkled with myrrh and aloes and wound tightly about the body of Jesus, swathing the limbs in many folds and layers, a small square being reserved as "napkin" for the head. The whole procedure was marked by haste, and the grave in Joseph's garden was chosen because it was close at hand. Thither, in the last rays of the sun, they carried the sacred body and laid it as the first occupant in a niche of the rock-hewn sepulchre.

The evangelists make no attempt to describe the emotion with which the two honorable councilors performed the burial rites and rolled, before leaving, a large boulder against the entrance of the tomb. But in the mind of one of them must have echoed the words of the dead Teacher, "As Moses lifted up the serpent in the wilderness, even so must the Son of man be lifted up, that whosoever believeth may in Him have eternal life"; and, "He that doeth truth cometh to the light, that his deeds may be manifest, that they are wrought in God."

II

How life and death in Thee
Agree!
Thou hadst a virgin womb
And tomb.
A Joseph did betroth
Them both.

With what haste, O my Jesus, Thou art lowered from the Cross and borne to the grave! The shadows of evening are stretched out, and the day goeth away. Before the sabbath breaks, Thy Body must be hidden out of sight; before the sun sets, O Sun of Righteousness, Thou must be underground. There is scant time for burial honors. Swiftly fly the hands of love, rich and fine are the linen and the spices; yet it is but a temporary entombment. But such as it is, it is most fitting for Thy short rest in the grave. Moreover, Thou hast already a better anointing. Mary of Bethany hath prepared Thy Body for the burying with ointment of spikenard very precious, the odor of which clings still to Thy head and feet, and will not yield to all the myrrh and aloes lavished on Thee after death. Most fitting, too, is Thy burial in another's grave. How could it be otherwise? What hast Thou to do with a sepulchre, to whom death does not properly belong? Therefore art Thou laid in the sepulchre of another, because Thou didst die for the salvation of others.

Thy short rest on Thy couch of rock, O Lord of life, has hallowed the graves of all Thy saints. Now there need be no more fear of death nor foreboding of the tomb. Now our graves are become to us what Joseph's was to him when the three days were past. It was a high honor to shelter even the dead Body of Jesus, but it was joy unspeakable and full of glory to find His sepulchre become the birthplace of life and immortality. O holier than Bethlehem, thou cave in Joseph's garden, cradle of glorious, heavenly life! If even the patriarchs of old rejoiced to be gathered to their people, and Joseph in Egypt charged the children of Israel to carry his body home and lay it in sacred soil, what must have been the emotions of this other Joseph at the thought of laying himself down where his risen Lord had lain! I see him walking in his garden, from which the Easter glow had never faded, and where

> Young men that no one knew went in and out
> With a far look in their eternal eyes.

261

I see him walking in his garden, and as he pauses before the sepulchre I hear him say, "O grave, where is thy victory?" And when his time came to die, how peacefully he fell asleep, knowing that his Lord had been before him and had prepared a place for him even in his grave, that sacred spot which had felt the stir of dead Limbs wakening, and from which the stone was now for ever rolled away.

III

For Rest in the Lord

O LORD JESUS CHRIST, Who for my sake didst not only suffer death, but wast laid in the tomb in order by Thy burial to hide my sins and hallow my grave: Grant that I may not dig up my sins again, but leave them buried in Thy tomb. By Thy rest in the grave give me the comfortable assurance that after this life my soul shall repose in God's hands, and my body sleep in the ground, and that at the last day I shall enter into Thine eternal rest. *Amen.*

For Burial With Christ

ALL HAIL, HOLY JESUS! Praise, honor, and glory be to Thee, O Christ, Who after Thou wast taken down from the Cross amid the grief of Thy friends, wast anointed with spices, wrapped in linen, and laid in another's tomb; Bury, I beseech Thee, all my senses, all my powers and affections in Thyself; so that, united to Thee by constraining love, I may become dead to all else but Thee, and may know and feel that Thou art the one only Redeemer of my soul, my chief and only God. O good Jesus, gracious Jesus! O my Hope, my Refuge, and my Salvation! Grant me complete mortification and renunciation of self. Extinguish in me all evil affections and lusts. *Amen.*

For Preparation for Death

O BLESSED LORD JESUS, Whose sacred Body, after Thou hadst finished in it the work of our redemption, was taken down from the Cross, and after a short repose in the sepulchre was raised again to a glorious immortality: Grant me, I beseech Thee, so frequently to renew in my mind the meaning of Thy grave, that I may be always prepared for my own; and so seriously to reflect on the consequences of a holy death, that every day I may learn to care less for this transitory life, and more for the eternal joys of Thy presence; Who with the Father and the Holy Ghost livest, One God, for ever and ever. *Amen.*

IV

"NOW SLEEPS THE LORD"

Now lies the Lord in a most quiet bed,
   Stillness profound
Steeps like a balm the wounded body wholly.
More still than the hushed night brooding around.
   The moon is overhead,
Sparkling and small, and somewhere a faint sound
Of water dropping in a cistern slowly.
Now lies the Lord in a most quiet bed.

Now rests the Lord in perfect loneliness.
One little grated window has the tomb,
  A patch of gloom
Impenetrable, where the moonbeams whiten
  And arabesque its wall
With leafy shadows, light as a caress.
The palms that brood above the garden brighten,
  But in that quiet room
Darkness prevails, deep darkness fills it all.
Now rests the Lord in perfect loneliness.

Now sleeps the Lord, crowned with ineffable peace.
Have they not peace to-night who feared Him, hated
  And hounded to His doom,
The red thirst of their vengeance being sated?
No, they still run about and bite the beard,
  Confer, nor cease
To tease the contemptuous Pilate, are afeared
Still of Him tortured, crushed, humiliated,
  Cold in a blood-stained tomb.
Now sleeps the Lord crowned with ineffable peace.

Now lies the Lord serene, august, apart,
That mortal life His mother gave Him ended.
  No word save one
Of Mary more, but gently as a cloud
On her perdurable silence has descended.

  Hush! In her heart
Which first felt the faint life stir in her Son,
  Perchance is apprehended
Even now dimly new mystery, grief less loud
Clamors, the Resurrection has begun.
Now lies the Lord serene, august, apart.

☩

O GRAVE, WHERE IS THY VICTORY?

Good Friday

39. THE WOMEN AT THE TOMB

I wait for the Lord, my soul doth wait and in His
word do I hope.
   My soul waiteth for the Lord more than they that
watch for the morning: I say, more than they that
watch for the morning.

Luke 23:54-56

(Matt. 27:61; Mark 15:47)

And it was the day of the Preparation, and the Sabbath drew on. And the women, who had come with Him out of Galilee, followed after and beheld the tomb, and how His body was laid. And they returned, and prepared spices and ointments. And on the sabbath they rested according to the commandment.

I

Though Joseph and Nicodemus had departed, the garden was not forsaken. Near the sepulchre lingered a little group of Galilean women, who had accompanied Jesus to Jerusalem. On Calvary they had kept their station near the cross with the sorrowful mother; later, when John took her to his home, they stood afar off with Jesus' acquaintances. They seem to have borne no active part in the descent from the cross and the burial; it would have been scarcely in accordance with Jewish manners for these women to assist the two councilors and their attendants. But now that all was over they might draw near unhindered. In the gathering shadows they sat "over against the sepulchre" with their tears and their memories—Mary of Magdala, out of whom the dead Master had cast seven demons; Joanna, the wife of Chuzas, Herod's steward, who together with others had ministered to Him out of her substance; and Mary, wife of Clopas and mother of James and Joses, a relative of the holy family.

Not only did sacred memories engage them, but in their hearts a plan of love was forming. They were not satisfied with the hasty entombment of their Lord. Notwithstanding the liberal supply of myrrh and aloes provided by Nicodemus, they longed to bring spices and ointments of their own for the beloved body and to bestow upon it such burial honors as it deserved. Promising one another to meet again at the sepulchre "very early in the morning the first day of the week," they hastened away, to spend what must have been for them the longest sabbath of their lives. The devotion of these holy women links Good Friday with Easter Day, the death and burial of Jesus with His resurrection. Indeed, these verses in Luke's gospel form the actual beginning of the Easter story. If we read them carefully, noting how the subject of the sentence is carried over into the following chapter—the names of the women are not given until we come to verse 10 of chapter xxiv—we shall see how the Passion narrative merges and forms a connected whole with the story of the Resurrection.

II

Drop, drop, slow tears,
And bathe those beauteous feet,
Which brought from heaven
The news and Prince of peace:
Cease not, wet eyes,
His mercies to intreat;
To cry for vengeance
Sin doth never cease:
In your deep floods
Drown all my faults and fears;
Nor let His eye
See sin, but through my tears.

O God, the Father of mercies, who didst not spare Thine own Son, but deliveredst Him up for us all! On this day of His death and burial I would sit with the Galilean women at His tomb and plead with Thee His holy life and precious death. Remember, I beseech Thee, His taking on Him the form of a servant and humbling Himself to be born of a Virgin. Remember His holy childhood and those quiet years of Nazareth. Remember how Thou didst declare Him at His Baptism to be Thy well beloved Son. Remember His victory over Satan and every evil will and way. Remember for good the days of His ministry. His speech with grace and with authority, His works of might and mercy, His patience and meekness, and His many prayers. O remember all His bodily pain and anguish of heart in the time of His Passion; how for the joy that was set before Him He endured the Cross, despising the shame; how He became obedient unto death. Call to mind His bloody sweat; the stripes and spitting, when Thou didst lay on Him the iniquity of us all; the scourge, the thorns, the nails, the spear; and that exceeding bitter cry when He gave up the ghost. Behold, now He is come to the end of His earthly course; He is laid, as at the first, in a cave and wrapped in the swaddling bands of death, all His beauty faded as a flower. He is become as a man that hath no strength, free among the dead. Lo, He is wholly yielded up to Thee and lies without stirring under Thy mighty hand. Accept, O Lord, I beseech Thee, this whole burnt offering and sacrifice as a sweet smelling savor, and have respect unto His offering as Thou hadst unto that of Abel. Let His death be precious in Thy sight. Thou who didst deliver Him for our offences, raise Him again for our justification. Do Thou highly exalt Him and set Him at Thy right hand and make His enemies His footstool. Let His perfect sacrifice avail also for me, O God of my salvation. God be merciful to me a sinner. Holy God, Holy and Mighty, Holy and Immortal, have mercy upon me.

For this Thy plenteous redemption I will offer up to Thee the sacrifice of praise continually, even the fruit of my lips giving thanks to Thy name. I offer to Thee a broken and a contrite heart, which Thou, O Lord, wilt not despise. I offer to Thee my soul and spirit: do Thou come and with Thy Son abide in me. I offer to Thee my body, a living sacrifice: let it be holy and acceptable in Thy sight. I offer to Thee my mortal life, with all my natural gifts and talents and all the bestowals of Thy grace: sanctify me wholly, that I may be Thine with all I am and all I have for ever. I offer to Thee my prosperity and my adversity, my joys and griefs. I offer to Thee myself, together with all my loved ones living and dead. Let me not sorrow overmuch for them that sleep in Jesus, nor mourn even as others who have no hope. O Christ, our Hope, even in the grave Thou art the Resurrection and the Life. Thou who didst die and rise again, that Thou mightest be Lord both of the dead and of the living! whether we live or die, Thou art our Lord; living or dying, have mercy upon us, O Lord!

Unto Him that loved us, and loosed us from our sins by His blood, and hath made us kings and priests unto God and His Father; to Him be glory and dominion for ever and ever. *Amen.*

III

A SHORT LITANY FOR GOOD FRIDAY *

Lord, have mercy.
Christ, have mercy.
Lord, have mercy.

Jesus, our Prophet,
Hear us, that we may hear Thee;
Jesus, our High Priest,
Plead for us, that we may plead in Thee.
Jesus, our King,
Reign over us, that we may reign with Thee,

---

*The Golden Litany (pp. 304-11) may be used instead.

By the trial before Caiaphas, Pilate, and Herod,
By Thy mocking by servants and soldiers,
By Thy rejection at the hands of Thy people, preferring a
robber,
By Thy scourging and crowning with thorns,
By Thy painful way to Golgotha,
  Have mercy upon us, and spare us.

By the wounds in Thy hands and feet,
By the title over Thy head,
By the reproaches of living and dying,
By Thy seven words on the Cross,
By Thy bowing the head and giving up the ghost,
  Have mercy upon us, and forgive us our sins.

By the miraculous signs attending Thy death,
By the good confession of the centurion,
By the spear-wound in Thy side,
By Thy descent from the Cross and Thy burial,
By Thy short rest in the tomb,
  Have mercy upon us, and grant us Thy peace.
OUR FATHER

A Thanksgiving for the Sufferings of Christ

O LORD JESUS CHRIST, Thou innocent and spot-
less Lamb of God, That takest away the sin of the
world! we thank Thee for Thy most holy sufferings
and death. O Thou perfect Sacrifice, Thou precious
Lamb, Thou patient Heart! how my sins have grieved
Thee! O sacred Head, how art thou wounded! O
sweetest Countenance, how art thou marred! O holy
Ears, what blasphemies must ye hear! O blessed
Hands, how are ye pierced! O holy Body, Temple of
God, how art thou torn and bruised! What can we

render Thee, Lord Jesus, for this Thine unspeakable goodness and mercy? Thanks be to Thee for Thy sacred wounds in hands and feet and side, and for the priceless treasure of Thy most precious Blood, through which we have redemption, even the forgiveness of sins. Thou, O God, hast accepted this Sacrifice of Thy dear Son, and wilt not again require it of us. Graciously accept us, therefore, and enable us to partake always of the precious benefits of Thy dear Son's death. *Amen.*

For the Desolate and Sorrowing

HAVE COMPASSION, O Lord, upon all who are mourning for those dear to them, and upon all who are lonely and desolate. Be Thou their Comforter and Friend; give them such earthly solace as Thou seest to be best for them, and bringing them to the fuller knowledge of Thy love, do Thou wipe away all their tears; for the sake of Jesus Christ our Lord. *Amen.*

IV

"THERE IS NOTHING MORE THAT THEY CAN DO"

There is nothing more that they can do
  For all their passionate care,
Those who sit in dust, the blessed few,
  And weep and rend their hair—

Peter, Thomas, Mary Magdalen,
  The Virgin unreproved,
Joseph and Nicodemus, foremost men,
  And John the well-beloved.

271

THE MAN OF SORROWS

Bring your finest linen and your spice,
    Swathe the sacred Dead,
Bind with careful hands and piteous eyes
    The napkin round His head:

Lay Him in the garden-rock to rest:
    Rest you the Sabbath length:
The Sun that went down crimson in the west
    Shall rise renewed in strength.

God Almighty shall give joy for pain,
    Shall comfort him who grieves:
Lo He with joy shall doubtless come again
    And with Him bring His sheaves.

✠

THANKS BE TO GOD, WHO GIVETH US THE VICTORY
THROUGH OUR LORD JESUS CHRIST

Easter Even

All that hate me whisper together against me: now that He lieth He shall rise up no more.

He that sitteth in the heavens shall laugh: the Lord shall have them in derision.

Matthew 27:62-66

Now on the morrow, which is the day after the Preparation, the chief priests and the Pharisees were gathered together unto Pilate, saying, Sir, we remember that that deceiver said while He was yet alive, After three days I rise again. Command therefore that the sepulchre be made sure until the third day, lest haply His disciples come and steal Him away, and say unto the people, He is risen from the dead: and the last error will be worse than the first. Pilate said unto them, Ye have a guard: go, make it as sure as ye can. So they went, and made the sepulchre sure, sealing the stone, the guard being with them.

I

Though the sabbath was a high day, it brought no rest for the members of the Sanhedrin. In the midst of their triumph some of them recalled the prediction of Jesus that He would rise from the dead on the third day. Imputing their own motives to others, they conceived the possibility that His disciples might secretly remove His body and give out that He had returned to life. If that were to happen the end of this affair would be worse than its beginning. The action of Joseph and Nicodemus, two distinguished colleagues of theirs, showed plainly that the cause of Jesus, far from being defeated, was gaining new and powerful adherents. They decided, therefore, to send a delegation to the governor with the request that he set a watch for three days about the sepulchre, in addition to which they would attach their official seal to the stone before the entrance. Not that they believed for one moment that Jesus' prediction would be fulfilled; seal and sentinels were intended not to prevent Jesus from rising, but His disciples from making it appear that He had risen. Hence they referred expressly to Him as a deceiver and to His teaching as a fraud.

The delegation found Pilate ready to grant their request. He offered them a guard of soldiers for the sepulchre, with the words, "Make it as sure as ye can." Here is the last of Pilate's cryptic sayings. Whether or not there was any intended mockery in his words, Matthew clearly understood them in this sense and wove them into his narrative, closing his account of the Passion with what is doubtless the most ironic sentence in literature—"So they went and made the sepulchre sure." As he wrote it there must have been a smile of triumph on his face.

II

I shall arise—let God know where!
Earth measured o'er from sea to sea
Affords not earth to bury me;

Dig the grave deep; roll up above
Sierras! yet the clod shall move,
Who lived and loved shall live and love!

Strong Son of God, Immortal Love! shut behind the
bolts and bars of death, Thou waitest for the morning. Even now the sun decketh himself as a bridegroom, and rejoiceth as a strong man to run a race.
But Thou wilt be up before him, our Sun of Righteousness, with healing in Thy wings. It is not possible
that Thou shouldest be holden of death. Like unto
Samson, bound with seven green withes and with new
ropes that were never used, Thou wilt break Thy
bonds like a thread, and as tow is broken when it
toucheth the fire. Nay, Thou wilt let Thyself out of
Thy prison, carrying away the doors of the gate upon
Thy shoulders, O Mighty God. Looking down upon
Thee locked in Thy tomb by the puny might of men,
He that sitteth in the heavens shall laugh; the Lord
shall have them in derision. When Thou wentest in to
raise up the young daughter of Jairus, saying, "She is
not dead, but sleepeth," they laughed Thee to scorn.
Now, while men say of Thee, "He is dead, and shall
rise up no more," Thy Father laugheth in the heavens.
Before another morning that heavenly laughter will
shake the earth, and roll away the stone from the
sepulchre, and cause the keepers to become as dead
men. Thou, His Isaac, His Laughter, shalt return again
from the dead; in Thee shall all nations of the earth be
blessed. The voice of rejoicing and salvation shall be in
the tabernacles of the righteous. Weeping may endure
for a night, but joy cometh in the morning.

O God, who canst do everything! O God, my exceeding joy! I will sing to Thee, I will praise Thee, I will bless Thee while I live, I will sing praise to Thee while I have my being. Let God arise, let His enemies be scattered: let them also that hate Him flee before Him. Like as the smoke vanisheth, so shalt Thou drive them away: and like as wax melteth at the fire, so let the ungodly perish at the presence of God: but let the righteous be merry and joyful before Him. I will sing unto the Lord as long as I live; and at life's close I will both lay me down in peace and sleep, for Thou, Lord, only makest me dwell in safety. When I awake, I shall be still with Thee. May Christ, the Son of the living God, have mercy upon us, and place us in the green and pleasant places of His own Paradise: and may the True Shepherd recognize us among His sheep. May we behold our Redeemer face to face, and for ever standing in His presence behold with blessed eyes the very Truth. Set among the companies of the blessed, may we enjoy the sweetness of Divine contemplation for ever. May songs and everlasting joy be upon our heads, and sorrow and sighing flee away.

O God of Hope, fill us with all joy and peace in believing, that we may abound in hope, through the power of the Holy Ghost.

III

Easter Vigil

GOD ALMIGHTY bless us, and of His mercy vouchsafe to defend us from all wickedness. *Amen.*

And may He who willed to enlighten this most holy night by the Resurrection of our Redeemer cleanse our minds from the darkness of our sins, and make them glisten with abundant virtues. *Amen.*

To the end that, striving to imitate the innocence of the newly-baptized, we may be enabled like the Wise Virgins to enter with shining lights into the chamber of that Bridegroom Whose Resurrection we are about to celebrate. *Amen.*

Abide With Us

ABIDE WITH US, abide with us until the morning. Let us enjoy Thy presence, let us be glad and rejoice in Thy Resurrection. The darkness deepens, the evening cometh fast. May our Sun, the Light eternal, Christ our God, show us the light of His countenance. With my soul will I desire Thee in the night: yea, with my spirit within me will I seek Thee early. Yet in the meanwhile wilt Thou come unto us, O Lord, because Thou art gracious, and wilt not tarry, because Thou art good. To Thee be glory, world without end. *Amen.*

Thanksgiving to Jesus Our Life

To jesus, the Life of our flesh,
Who quickeneth whom He willeth:
To Jesus, the Life of our soul,
Who came that we might live more abundantly:
To Jesus, the Life of His Church,

Who loved her and gave Himself for her:
Let all mankind in earth and in paradise,
Reconciled by His death, and saved by His life,
    Give glory and honor, worship and praise,
    Now and for ever and ever. *Amen.*

Final Prayer

THE GOD OF PEACE, That brought again from the dead our Lord Jesus Christ, that Great Shepherd of the sheep, through the blood of the everlasting covenant, make me perfect in every good work to do His will, working in me that which is well pleasing in His sight, through Jesus Christ; to whom be glory for ever and ever. *Amen.*

IV

EASTER EVEN

There is nothing more that they can do
    For all their rage and boast:
Caiaphas with his blaspheming crew,
    Herod with his host;

Pontius Pilate in his judgment hall,
    Judging their Judge and his,
Or he who led them all and passed them all,
    Arch-Judas with his kiss.

The sepulchre made sure with ponderous stone,
    Seal that same stone, O priest:
It may be thou shalt block the Holy One
    From rising in the east.

"MAKE IT AS SURE AS YE CAN"

Set a watch about the sepulchre
　　To watch on pain of death:
They must hold fast the stone if One should stir
　　And shake it from beneath.

God Almighty, He can break a seal,
　　And roll away a stone:
Can grind the proud in dust who would not kneel,
　　And crush the mighty one.

☩

THE THIRD DAY HE ROSE AGAIN FROM THE DEAD.
HALLELUJAH!

ANIMA CHRISTI

Soul of Christ, be my sanctification;
Body of Christ, be my salvation;
Blood of Christ, fill all my veins;
Water of Christ's side, wash out my stains;
Passion of Christ, my comfort be;
O good Jesu, listen to me;
In Thy wounds I fain would hide,
Ne'er to be parted from Thy side;
Guard me, should the foe assail me;
Call me when my life shall fail me;
Bid me come to Thee above,
With Thy saints to sing Thy love,
*   World without end. Amen.*

The Golden Litany

LIFE AND PASSION OF OUR
LORD JESUS CHRIST

Lord, have mercy upon us.

Christ, have mercy upon us: and grant us strength of soul,
inward and outward, that we may serve Thee according to
the pleasure of Thy will.

O Lord God, Father of Heaven,

By Thy Heavenly power have mercy upon us.

O Son of God, Redeemer of the world,

O Holy Ghost, One God, with the Father and the Son,

Have mercy upon us.

O Lord God, by Thine uncreate and undivided Trinity,

By Thy divine Being and Nature,

By Thine Infinite Glory and beauty,

By Thy Self, and all Goodness that Thou beholdest in Thy
Self,

By Thy Creation of Heaven and earth, and all things that are
in them,

By Thy Goodness in the creation of Man in Thine own Image
and Likeness,

By that great Love, whereby Thou didst elect to restore man
when he fell,

By that ineffable Love, whereby Thou chosest Mary most pure
Virgin to be Thy Mother,

By that meek Affection and Love which drew Thee from the
bosom of the Father unto the womb of the Virgin,

For that Thou didst not loathe to take upon Thee the Frailty
of man for our sins,

For Thy holy Nativity, wherein Thou didst vouchsafe to be
born of a woman,

By that cold Manger which Thou layest in, wrapped in poor clothes, and fed with maiden's milk,

By the great Joy of the Shepherds, who worshiped Thee lying in a manger,

For Thy painful Circumcision, and Shedding of Thy precious Blood, and by the Virtue of Thy holy Name Jesus, and all Thy blessed Names,

For the blessed Oblation of Thyself to Thy Father in the Temple,

For Thy Flight into Egypt, and all that Thou didst suffer there,

For Thy coming again from Egypt to Nazareth, and Thy Obedience to Thy Father and Mother,

For Thy lowly and meek Conversation, for three and thirty years on earth,

For Thy most holy Meditations, Words, and Works of mercy,

For Thy holy Baptism, and the glorious Manifestation of the Holy Trinity,

For Thy holy Fasting, Meditation, and Temptation,

For the Thirst, Hunger, Cold, and Heat which Thou didst suffer,

For Thy Heaviness, Labor, and Weariness,

For the Detraction and evil Words wherewith Thine enemies reviled Thee,

For Thy Watching and Prayers,

For Thy wholesome Doctrine, and mighty Resistance, whereby Thou gavest no place to Thine enemies,

For the wonderful Signs and Miracles which Thou wroughtest,

For Thy holy Tears and lowly Entrance into Jerusalem on Palm Sunday,

By that fervent and charitable Desire, that Thou hadst to redeem us,

By that great lowliness which Thou showedst in washing the feet of Thy disciples, and of Judas who betrayed Thee,

For Thy most noble and worthy Institution of the Sacrament of Thy most precious Body and Blood,

For the profound Love, whereby Thou didst permit St. John the Evangelist to rest upon Thy breast at Thy Supper,

For the Peace which Thou gavest to Thy disciples,

For Thy holy Words and Sermons,

For the great inward Heaviness which Thou hadst when Thou prayedst to Thy Father in the Garden,

By the virtue of Thy holy Prayer which Thou prayedst there three times,

For Thy fearful Dread of Thy death,

For that Agony wherein Thou offeredst Thyself willingly in obedience to Thy Almighty Father, and for Thy Bloody Sweat,

By that great Meekness whereby Thou didst will to be comforted by an Angel,

By Thy mighty and victorious Courage, wherewith Thou wentest to meet them that sought to kill Thee,

By Thy fearful Taking, when the Jews laid their hands violently upon Thee,

For Thy great Goodness, in that Thou refusedst not the kiss of Judas, Thy betrayer, and didst heal the ear of Malchus that Peter smote off,

For those holy Bonds wherewith Thou wast bound, and led as a prisoner: and the opprobrious Words that Thou didst suffer all that night,

For the Blow Thou didst endure in the presence of the High Priest Annas, and other shame done to Thee,

For that Love and Charity that Thou hadst when Thou wert brought bound before Caiaphas the High Priest,

By the false Witnesses, and Thine unrighteous Condemnation,

By the Spitting upon Thee, and the Scorning of Thee,

By the Buffetings and sore Strokes given to Thee,

By the Binding and Blindfolding of Thine Holy eyes, by all the Shame and Reproof that Thou didst suffer all that night,

For that merciful Look wherewith Thou beheldest Peter, and for all that Labor and Torment, secret and unknown, which Thou didst suffer all that night,

By Thy Presentation before Pilate, and the Accusations that the Jews made against Thee,

For the Contempt and Mockery that Thou didst suffer when Herod arrayed Thee in a gorgeous robe, and sent Thee again to Pilate,

For all the Shame, Labor, Upbraiding, and Reproof which Thou didst suffer going from one Judge to another,

For Thy great Patience and Stillness,

For the shameful Stripping of Thy clothes, and the Binding of Thy most holy Body to a pillar,

For Thy Scourgings and cruel Beatings,

For Thine innumerable Wounds, and the plenteous Shedding of Thy Blood,

For all Thy Pain, Sorrow, Cold, and Shivering,

For the purple Garment, and the Crown of thorns violently pressed upon Thy head,

For the great Pain that Thou didst suffer in Thy Head, when it was smitten on the crown of thorns,

By the scornful Worshiping of the Jews and their Salutation, when they said, "Hail, King of the Jews,"

By the Spitting on Thy divine Face and the cruel Beatings,

For that Heaviness of Heart which Thou hadst when Pilate brought Thee forth before the multitude of the people, wearing the crown of thorns and the purple robe, and said to them, "Behold, the Man,"

For that fearful Sentence of death, and shameful Leading to the Mount of Calvary,

For Thy great Love shewed to us when Thou borest Thy heavy Cross upon Thy shoulders, to the place where Thou sufferedst Thy most painful Passion; and the Labor, Anguish, Slanders, and Beatings Thou didst suffer by the way,

For all Thy bloody Steps, as Thou didst go to Thy death,

By the great Weariness that Thou hadst in Thy shoulders, bearing the Cross until Thou fellest down,

By the great Compassion of Thy Heart, when bearing the Cross, Thou didst meet the Holy Women sorrowing and making lamentation,

By Thy Heaviness of soul, and the Going up to the Mount of Calvary, where Thou wast crucified,

By the Stripping of Thy Clothes to Thy great shame in the sight of all the people,

By that cold Sitting that Thou satest, piteously full of wounds, so abiding until Thy Cross was ready,

For those sore and painful Steps that Thou madest going to Thy Cross,

For Thy great Anguish, Mournings, and Weepings,

For the great Stretching of Thy sinews, and veins, and all Thy members,

By the Nailing of Thy Right Hand, and Shedding of Thy precious Blood,

By the Nailing of Thy Left Hand, and Thy most holy Wound, and precious Blood,

For the Nailing of Thy most holy Feet, and by the precious Blood flowing out of them,

For the Lifting up of Thy most holy Body on the Cross, and the sore Bruising thereof that gave to all parts of Thy Body an incredible pain,

For the Heaviness of Thy Heart, and all the powers of Thy Soul,

For the Parting of Thy Garments, and the Casting lots upon Thy seamless coat,

For Thy great Love whereby Thou didst hang alive upon the Cross three hours,

For those opprobrious and scornful Words, which hanging on the Cross, Thou heardest spoken unto Thee,

For the Blasphemy, Sorrow and Confusion that Thou didst suffer on the Cross,

For all the Pain that, being strained upon the Cross, Thou didst suffer in Thy Hands and Feet and all Thy Members,

For that wonderful Charity when Thou prayedst Thine Almighty Father for Thine enemies,

For Thy tender Mercy in that Thou didst promise Paradise to the Penitent Thief,

For the tender Care which Thou hadst for Thy Mother in Thy torments, commending her to Thy well-beloved disciple St. John,

For that great and piteous Cry which Thou madest to Thy Father,

For those holy Tears, which Thou sheddest on the Cross, and in all Thy Life-time,

For Thy Thirst and Tasting of Gall and Vinegar,

For all those holy Words that Thou spakest on the Cross, and in all Thy Life,

For that piteous Cry in which Thou commendedst Thy Soul to Thy Father,

By the Departing of Thy holy Soul from Thy blessed Body,

By the Resting of Thy most blessed Head upon Thy Breast,

By the Bitterness of Thy Death, and the intolerable pains wherewith Thy Heart brake,

By the Opening of Thy Side with a spear, and the flowing out of Thy most precious Blood,

By that most precious Blood and Water, that ran out of Thy most holy Heart,

For that great Mercy which Thou showedst to the Centurion beneath Thy Cross, and all Thy mercies which Thou hast ever shown unto us.

For the Taking down of Thy most holy Body from the Cross, and the Solemn Burial thereof amid the great Lamentation of Thy friends,

For all Thy painful Labors, Weariness, Sorrow, and Heaviness, which Thou didst suffer from the day of Thy Nativity unto the hour that Thy Soul departed from Thy Body,

For Thy glorious Resurrection in body and in soul,

For that special Grace, when Thou didst appear in a glorious Body, after Thy Resurrection, to Mary Magdalene, to the other women, and to Thy disciples,

For Thy wonderful and glorious Ascension,

For Thy divine Sending of the Holy Ghost the Comforter to Thy disciples,

For Thy glory and the divine Majesty and Virtues of Thy holy Name, save us and govern us, now and ever, and

For the Love, that dwelt both in Thy Manhood and Thy Godhead,

For that Joy whereby Thou hast fruition in Thyself,

For Thyself and all Goodness and Merits that Thou beholdest in Thyself,

Have mercy upon us.

Let us pray.

Succor us, most sweet Jesu, in that fearful day of Thy most strict Judgment, and grant us in this transitory life all things necessary to the health of our bodies and our souls, and that this life ended we may live with Thee in joy everlasting; Who livest and reignest God for ever and ever. *Amen.*

INDEX OF
Prayers *and* Verse

INDEX OF PRAYERS AND VERSE

291